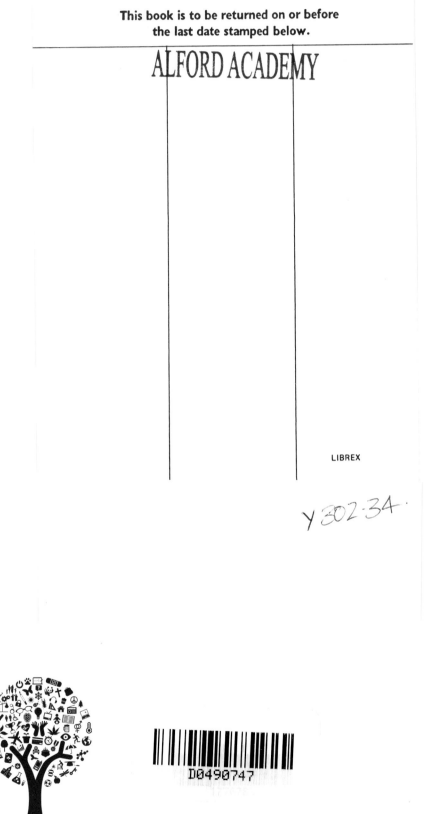

D0490747

Independence Educational Publishers

First published by Independence Educational Publishers

The Studio, High Green

Great Shelford

Cambridge CB22 5EG

England

© Independence 2019

Copyright

Photocopy licence

ISBN-13: 978 1 86168 810 1

Printed in Great Britain

Zenith Print Group

Contents

Introduction

RELATIONSHIPS is Volume 354 in the **ISSUES** series. The aim of the series is to offer current, diverse information about important issues in our world, from a UK perspective.

ABOUT RELATIONSHIPS

In today's society education on healthy relationships is very important. In this brand new title in the issues series, we look at different types of relationships, from families, to friends, to dating. It also looks at the benefits of stable relationships and how to recognise if a relationship is unhealthy.

OUR SOURCES

Titles in the **ISSUES** series are designed to function as educational resource books, providing a balanced overview of a specific subject.

The information in our books is comprised of facts, articles and opinions from many different sources, including:

◆ Newspaper reports and opinion pieces

◆ Website factsheets

◆ Magazine and journal articles

◆ Statistics and surveys

◆ Government reports

◆ Literature from special interest groups.

A NOTE ON CRITICAL EVALUATION

Because the information reprinted here is from a number of different sources, readers should bear in mind the origin of the text and whether the source is likely to have a particular bias when presenting information (or when conducting their research). It is hoped that, as you read about the many aspects of the issues explored in this book, you will critically evaluate the information presented.

It is important that you decide whether you are being presented with facts or opinions. Does the writer give a biased or unbiased report? If an opinion is being expressed, do you agree with the writer? Is there potential bias to the 'facts' or statistics behind an article?

ASSIGNMENTS

In the back of this book, you will find a selection of assignments designed to help you engage with the articles you have been reading and to explore your own opinions. Some tasks will take longer than others and there is a mixture of design, writing and research-based activities that you can complete alone or in a group.

FURTHER RESEARCH

At the end of each article we have listed its source and a website that you can visit if you would like to conduct your own research. Please remember to critically evaluate any sources that you consult and consider whether the information you are viewing is accurate and unbiased.

Useful Websites

www.esrc.ukri.org

www.childandfamilyblog.com

www.cardiff.ac.uk

www.cypnow.co.uk

www.exposure.org.uk

www.healthyrespect.co.uk

www.independent.co.uk

www.inews.co.uk

www.natcen.ac.uk

www.ons.gov.uk

www.rapecrisis.org.uk

www.sheffield.ac.uk

www.tcsnetwork.co.uk

www.teenbreathe.co.uk

www.telegraph.co.uk

www.theconversation.com

www.theguardian.com

www.thehideout.org.uk

www.thinkuknow.co.uk

www.unbiased.co.uk

www.warwick.ac.uk

www.yougov.co.uk

www.young.scot

Milestones: Journeying into adulthood

We used to think of getting married and having children as some of life's most important milestones. How are some of the modern markers of adulthood – from working life to living arrangements – changing?

For many young adults in the UK, their social media pages are full of baby pictures and wedding-day snaps from friends and acquaintances they've grown up with. Such events have traditionally been celebrated as the key milestones of early adulthood. When do these life events typically happen, and what are the other modern markers of adulthood, in work and family life?

Age 18: Legally an adult

The law gives children more rights and responsibilities as they grow up. From as young as eight in Scotland, or ten in the rest of the UK, they can be held responsible for criminal behaviour – although the Scottish Parliament is currently considering raising the age of criminal responsibility to 12 years old.

Teenagers get more rights as they get older – for example, they can begin doing 'light work' part-time from the age of 13 or 14 (depending on which part of the UK they live in). From the age of 16 they are legally able to consent to sexual activity, and from 17 they can start driving.

But it's not until their 18th birthday (or, in some circumstances, earlier in Scotland) that children become adults in the eyes of the law. Adults can enter into legal contracts, leave home, and take on debt. They're also able to buy alcohol, smoke, get married without their parents' permission, and vote in UK Parliamentary elections.

Age 23: Moving out of your parents' home

In 2017, the first age at which more than 50% of young people had left the parental home was 23. Two decades earlier, more than 50% of 21-year-olds had already left home.

Both men and women are living with their parents for longer than they did 20 years earlier, but it's young men who are more likely to stay with their parents than young women. In 2017, of men aged 18 to 34 years old, 37% lived with their parents, compared with 26% of women in the same age group.

There are a few possible reasons for this: women have traditionally moved in with a partner at younger ages than men; women are also more likely to go to university; and there is some evidence that, early in their careers at least, women have been known to earn more than men.

In 1997, the most common living arrangement for young adults was as a couple with one or more children (29% of 18- to 34-year-olds). By 2017, there were more young adults living with their parents (32% of 18- to 34-year-olds). During this period, the costs of both renting and buying homes have increased, and the average ages of getting married and having children have risen. These factors, combined

with the rise in the number of people staying in education and not in full-time work, may be factors in encouraging young adults to remain living with their parents.

Age 27: Moving in with a partner

The age at which people move in with a partner has not changed much over the last couple of decades and has fluctuated between 26 and 27.

More than 50% of 27-year-olds were living with a partner in 2017. Women are more likely to move in with their partner earlier than men, with more than 50% of 26-year-old women living with a partner. The first age at which more than half of men are living with a partner is 28.

Age 29: Having a baby

The age at which women have their first child has been increasing for more than 40 years. In 2016, the average age of a first-time mother was 29 – two years later than it was in 1997.

It's not possible to produce a figure for the average age of first-time fathers, as when births are registered, fathers aren't asked whether they have any children already. We do know the average age of all fathers in England and Wales is around three years higher than for all mothers. In 2017, the average age of all fathers (not just first-time fathers) in England and Wales was 33.4 years, compared with 31.5 years in 1997.

Age 32: Getting married

Many people used to see marriage as a precursor to having children. In the UK today, people in their 20s are more likely to have children than be married, with the average age of first-time marriage increasing in 2015 to 33 for men and 31 for women (up from ages 30 and 27, respectively in 1997).

In 1979, in England and Wales, 94% of 34-year-old women, and 88% of 34-year-old men, had ever been married. By 2015, this figure had fallen to 51% of 34-year-old women and 41% of 34-year-old men.

There are numerous reasons for the changes in the timing and number of marriages in the UK. With weddings rising in price and house prices increasing, the cost of setting up family life has increased considerably.

We've also seen changing attitudes to marriage itself through changes in society, religion and cultural norms, including a reduced parental expectation to marry in your twenties.

Age 34: Owning your own home

The age at which people own their own home is continuing to rise: it is not until the age of 34 that more than 50% of people

Percentage of people living with parents by age, UK, 1997 and 2017

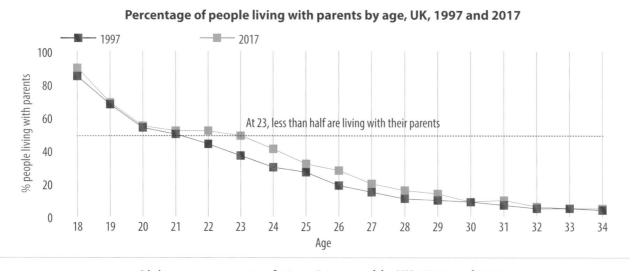

At 23, less than half are living with their parents

Living arrangements of 18- to 34-year-olds, UK, 1997 and 2017

1997	2017
Couple with 1+ children **28.8%**	Living with parents **32%**
Living with parents **25.5%**	Couple with 1+ children **21.8%**
Couple, no children **19.6%**	Couple, no children **19%**
Other **9.4%**	Other **14.5%**
Alone **8.6%**	Alone **5.4%**
Lone parent with 1+ children **5.3%**	Lone parent with 1+ children **4%**
Two or more unrelated adults **2.8%**	Two or more unrelated adults **3.3%**

Note: "Other" includes people in multi-family households (these contain at least two families). The families may be related. "Other" may also contain those who are the head of the family unit or the partner of the head of the family unit, but not the head of the household, or the partner or cohabitee of the head of the household. It may also include those in a one-person family but who live with others in their household. Data do not include students living in halls of residence.

Percentage of birth cohorts married by the year of their 34th birthday, England and Wales, 1934 to 2016

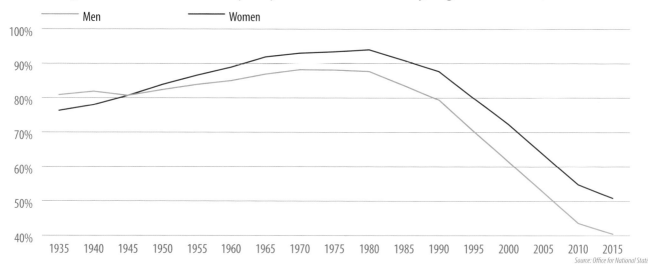

Source: Office for National Statistics

live in a home they own (based on the age of household reference persons, individuals within a household who act as a reference person for all individuals in the household). In 1997, the youngest age at which more than 50% of people were homeowners was 26.

Over the last 20 years, renting (from both the private and social sector) has become more common across all but the oldest age groups. The most substantial change has been for those aged 25 to 34 – in 2018, among this age group 55% were renting, up from 35% in 1998.

Over this period, there are many factors that could be contributing towards falling rates of home ownership,

including the introduction of stricter mortgage lending rules introduced after the 2008 recession and the rising cost of an entry-level property.

In 1993, the average house price was 4.9 times the average household salary of a household headed by a 16- to 24-year-old. In 2016, it was 8.2 times (a decline from its peak of 11.2 times in 2007).

18 February 2019

Getting married

By Nick Green

Why get married? Of course, because you love each other. But what some cohabiting couples don't consider is that there are additional legal and financial benefits to being married. Besides the confetti, food, flowers, favours and gifts, you're also entering into a major contract. Marriage and civil partnerships bring with them a number of responsibilities, but also several perks.

Here are key financial and legal points to consider when tying the knot:

- The initial cost of marriage
- Financial perks of being married
- The marriage allowance
- How does marriage affect children?
- How being married affects your will
- Marriage and pensions
- Marriage and separation
- Civil partnerships.

The cost of marriage

Big weddings are notoriously expensive – the average cost in the UK is over £20,000. But if that's all that puts you off getting married, think again. The legal benefits and safeguards of being in a married couple are worthwhile in themselves, and a low-key ceremony needn't break the bank. It's just as romantic to use your hard-earned joint savings as a deposit on your first home together.

If you do dream of a lavish white wedding, then you may need to start saving or investing for it even before you meet your future spouse. (Just don't mention it on the first date.)

The financial perks of marriage

Marriage can leave couples significantly better off over time, after the wedding has been paid for. One advantage is that spouses can transfer money and assets between them other tax-free, which can reduce your overall tax bill.

You also have more financial protection if you were to separate, or if one of you were to die. For instance, if you have a joint mortgage but are not married, you wouldn't automatically inherit your partner's share of the home if they were to die. Being married, on the other hand, means all assets are owned jointly between you. Similarly, if an unmarried couple split up, each partner keeps what is legally theirs (which may be very harsh on a low-earning partner). But if a married couple divorce, assets can be shared more fairly.

There is also a small marriage allowance that can save you income tax. The lower-earning spouse can transfer up to £1,190 of their personal allowance to the higher-earner, thus reducing their tax bill by up to £238.

Are married parents better for children?

Whether you're married or not, as biological or adoptive parents, you both have a parental responsibility to support your children financially.

Parental responsibility is the legal right to make decisions about the child's life, such as their name, education, home, health, religious upbringing and money set aside for them. Furthermore, anyone married to the mother has this parental responsibility – even if unrelated to the child. There are, however, other ways that you can get parental responsibility without marrying.

Does getting married affect my will?

When you get married, your previous will becomes invalid and you need to write a new one. If you don't, your entire estate will automatically be left to your spouse, which can mean that your children (including any from previous relationships) don't receive any inheritance.

On the other hand, if you're not married, your partner won't get anything if you die, unless your will specifies that they should. And if you've got a mortgage together, they will be fully responsible for it if you die. Even worse, if there are other claims on your share of it (such as from your children) then your partner may lose the home itself. A solicitor can help you draw up a will.

There are yet more savings to be had when it comes to inheritance tax. When one of you dies, any money or assets passed on are free from inheritance tax if you're married.

What about our pensions?

When you're married, you may be entitled to your spouse's State Pension after they die, depending on their level of National Insurance contributions. Note that it doesn't automatically entitle you to any of your spouse's workplace pension, or death-in-service benefits. For that, each spouse must name the other as the nominated beneficiary of the pension. Take particular care if you remarry, as old pension pots may still have your ex-spouse named as beneficiary.

What happens if we separate?

If you separate and you're not married, you're not entitled to anything you don't jointly own. Furthermore, it can be difficult to prove joint ownership, and this will probably require legal advice.

When you're married, things are a lot simpler. When you divorce, all the assets of the marriage are treated as joint assets, so you have a better chance of a fair settlement.

Some couples choose to sign a prenuptial agreement before they get married (or a postnuptial after the wedding) to outline what will happen if they decide to split. It can offer you protection if you want to make sure your spouse can't claim against some of your family's assets if you divorce. You can get a solicitor to help you draw these agreements up.

Is this all the same for civil partnerships?

If you're in a same-sex relationship, you can either get married or form a civil partnership. A civil partnership is almost legally identical to marriage, so all of the above still stands.

18 January 2019

Millennials don't want to get married

By Tanyaradzwa Mwamuka

Civil partnership is a term usually associated with same-sex couples. It was, until 2013, the only real option for same sex couples for legalising the status of their relationship. 2013 was when same-sex marriage was legalised in the UK. Fast forward five years and something new has been brought onto the market. Civil partnership is back, but this time for mixed couples too. Most instant reactions are questioning why. If civil partnerships have the same legal rights as a marriage, then what's the point?

It could be that marriage can be seen to be religious. Whilst the UK is considered a Christian country, in this day and age we are in reality, in a melting pot of varying religions. Though 50 years ago, the majority of White Britain would have identified as committed Christians, now, there seems to be a growing number of atheists or at the very least non-practising Christians.

Ms Steinfeld and Mr Keidan accidently become campaigners for the civil partnerships for mixed-sex couples. Having had 130,000 people sign their petition after a four-year campaign, they tasted success when The Supreme Court ruled in their favour this year. The implementation of this will not come into action until 2019 in England and Wales, but for them it certainly is a step in the right direction.

To get a real understanding of why civil partnership has become available to mixed couples, we have to look at the legal differences between cohabitation, civil partnership (for both mixed and same sex-couples) and marriage in the UK.

What is a marriage?

Marriage has varying definitions across the world and in different cultures. It is commonly seen as a social and ritualistic union between two people. It establishes obligations between the spouses and resulting children (whether biological or adoptive) and other extended relatives. When getting married you can choose between a civil or religious marriage. There are however some religious marriages that will not be recognised without a civil marriage. If you have a joint bank account, the money becomes joint property regardless of who puts money into the account, which becomes important on death of a spouse or on separation of the couple. Marriage also affects parental responsibility for example, if you are the husband of child's birth mother you automatically have parental responsibility.

What is a civil partnership?

Civil partnerships were introduced to give same-sex couples a way of obtaining similar legal and financial security, that marriage did. To my amazement this has only been a legislation since 2004, and in 2013 new legislation allowed the choice of marriage in England, Wales and Scotland. Unlike marriage, you cannot bring a civil partnership to an end until it has lasted for at least one year. Much like a marriage the same banking rules apply to civil partnerships. Civil partnerships also allow the exemption of inheritance tax.

Why civil partnership over marriage?

Religion was the main reason people were against marriage, and yes that is certainly true for many people are getting married outside of a church, minister or the traditional Christian values. But even then, religion couldn't be the sole or even the most important reason to want civil partnership, surely. As I began to investigate it became clear people had issue not only with the religious link but the legacy of gender imbalance and roles which were routed with the traditions of marriage. Many women and men don't like the idea of marriage because of the sense of ownership that comes with it.

When dissecting the rituals, it's easy to see why people think this. Firstly, the suitor must ask for permission from the bride's father for her hand in marriage and in many traditions a price for the bride is agreed upon; in my own culture this is called lobola. From the modern perspective the idea of transferring ownership from father to husband, certainly seems archaic. The bride as a prize makes it almost seem like the women is a commodity being purchased. This ideology of transfer of possession can be interpreted within weddings in the ceremony itself, when the father walks his daughter down the aisle 'to give her away' to her future husband.

Within the marriage, historically, the husband is the head of the house and decision maker and the sentiment of a wife respecting her husband trickles down as friendly advice from mother to daughter and other female elders. An example of this sense of ownership is shown in the form of marital rape only coming into existence in recent years. Historically, as a woman you were obliged to provide your husband with sex, without consent from the other spouse being strictly needed. Currently, in modern laws, consent is essential and whether non-consensual sexual intercourse happens violently or non-violently it is considered marital rape. Whilst respect of one another is certainly good for a union, the emphasis on the woman in the marriage to uphold this rather than the man is an example of the gender inequality and imbalance which many modern couples see only civil partnership can resolve.

The Steinfeld-Keidan couple argued saying that 'the legacy of marriage… treated women as property for centuries…

we want to raise our children as equal partners and feel civil partnership – a modern, symmetrical institution – sets the best example for them'

With this to consider, you would think just not getting married would be enough.

Wrong; whilst marriage may not be an option for many, simply living together isn't either due to the lack of clarity of legal status cohabitation comes with.

Rights as cohabiters

Living together with a partner sometimes referred to as cohabitation doesn't actually have a legal definition. Many couples are disappointed on separation or death of partner to find they don't have many, if at all any legal, financial and parental rights. Civil partnership and marriage offers legal securities which cohabitation does not. At best, a cohabitation contract can be formed outlining obligations and rights of each partner, but there isn't clarity about whether this can be legally enforced. In terms of finances, if you have separate accounts, neither has access to each other's accounts. If you have joint accounts however, the money belongs to both of you. If only one of you however, has deposited money, then it becomes difficult for the partner who hasn't, to claim any of the money – which differs to marriage and civil partnership where you are entitled regardless.

For me, I don't necessarily see marriage the way many modern millennials do (perhaps I'm too much of a traditionalist). Some of the rituals dating back may very well be archaic for this time and age, but I choose which aspects of marriage I wish to celebrate and since there isn't an exact set of rules, I see no problem in exchanging out-of-date traditions for ones that suit me. Nonetheless, having the option for civil partnerships certainly makes sense and allows those not for marriage, an incredibly important thing: choice.

October 2018

These are your legal rights if you live with your partner but are not married

46 percent of people who cohabit think they are in a common-law marriage.

By Claire Schofield

Almost half of unmarried couples who live together mistakenly believe they share the same rights as couples who have tied the knot, research has found.

According to a survey by the National Centre for Social Research, 46 per cent of people who cohabit think they are in a common-law marriage. Experts are now warning that this misconception can increase the risk of severe financial hardship in the event of a break-up.

'No legal status'

Cohabiting couples account for the fastest growing type of household in England and Wales, according to a survey by the National Centre for Social Research.

However, simply living together grants 'no general legal status' to couples, meaning that in the event of a separation, they are not protected by the same rights as those who are married, or in a civil partnership.

Anne Barlow, family law and policy professor at the University of Exeter, which commissioned the study, explained, 'The number of opposite-sex cohabiting couple families with dependent children has more than doubled in the last decade, yet whilst people's attitudes towards marriage and cohabitation have shifted, policy has failed to keep up with the times.

'The result is often severe financial hardship for the more vulnerable party in the event of separation, such as women who have interrupted their career to raise children.'

A common misconception

Of those who took part in the survey, only 41 per cent were aware that there is no common-law marriage between cohabiting couples, with more than half of households with children believing that unmarried couples shared the same rights as those who are married.

Singles were most aware of the law, with only 39 per cent believing a common-law marriage existed, while more men (49 per cent) than women (44 per cent) mistakenly believed they were in a common-law marriage.

Professor Barlow said, 'It's absolutely crucial that we raise awareness of the difference between cohabitation, civil partnership and marriage, and any differences in rights that come with each.'

What are your rights if you live together, but are not married?

If you live together as a couple but are not married, you can formalise aspects of your status with a partner by drawing up a legal agreement, known as a cohabitation contract, or living together agreement.

UK Divorce Statistics

• According to the Office of National Statistics, there were **106,959** divorces of opposite-sex couples in 2016 in England and Wales. This is an increase of **5.8%** compared to 2015.

• However, divorce rates were **down over 20%** compared to 2003 and 2004.

• 112 same-sex couples were divorced in 2016; of these **78% were female couples**.

• The average age of divorcees rose to **46 for men** and **44 for women**, the highest these numbers have been on record.

• The average duration of marriages ending in divorce reached **12 years** – the second-highest figure on record. The last, and only other time, this figure was 12 years or longer was in 1972.

Source: iNews

This outlines the rights and obligations of each partner towards each other, and can include a series of legally enforceable agreements on specific matters, says Citizens Advice.

Within this agreement, couples can set out what would happen in the event of a separation, ensuring that neither party would lose out financially.

Cohabiting couples have no financial responsibility to each other if they separate, meaning you have no legal obligation to provide your partner with financial support.

If one partner owns the property you share, they are legally responsible for any bills, contracts, loans and credit cards taken out. The other partner has no legal responsibility for these things.

However, your partner may be considered liable for some outgoings, such as council tax, if he or she has been living in the property for a substantial period of time, although this is an exception.

Couples are advised to discuss who will pay what before they move in together, and for this to be set out in a cohabitation agreement to avoid financial losses if the relationship ends.

Additionally, cohabiting couples who start a family together cannot claim spousal support if the relationship breaks down, although in England and Wales parents have a financial responsibility to their children through the Government's Child Maintenance Service.

22 January 2019

Common-law marriage - a peculiarly persistent myth

There's no single way of 'doing' family in modern Britain: family life and personal relationships have changed considerably over the last few decades – from the introduction of same-sex marriage, to a marked increase in the number of mixed-race couples, or a rising tide of flat-sharing and young adults moving back in with their parents. Nowadays, cohabiting couples (both opposite and same-sex couples) are the fastest growing type of family, more than doubling from 1.5 million families in 1996 to 3.3 million families in 2017, with 15% of dependent children living in cohabiting couple families.[1]

While British society is evolving, policy is not always keeping pace with these changes; in England and Wales, cohabitants have no legal status and, therefore, no automatic rights in most circumstances – especially if the relationship comes to an end. For example, if one partner dies there's no right for the other to inherit part of their estate – regardless of how long they have lived together and even if they had children together. Equally, there is no exemption for tax purposes and no legal duty to support the partner financially.

Yet almost half of us (46%) living in England and Wales are unaware that this is the case and think that an unmarried cohabiting couple have a 'common-law marriage' with the same legal rights as a married couple, according to the latest British Social Attitudes Survey. This figure is largely unchanged since 2005.

The data also show that people living in households with children are significantly more likely to think that common-law marriage exists than those in households with no children (55% vs 41%) and singles (39%). Worryingly, cohabitants (48%) are no more clued up than married people (49%).

Misperceptions like this can have very real negative implications for people's lives and the decisions they take. Cohabitants may face financial hardship and even losing their home if the relationship breaks down. Additionally, we know that the lack of legal rights for cohabitants affects particular groups disproportionately, particularly women and children, as women remain more likely to put careers on hold while raising children and become financially dependent on their partners.

The recent introduction of civil partnerships for heterosexual couples will offer an alternative to couples who wish to form a legal union without entering a traditional marriage. However, as around half of cohabitants don't know about their lack of legal status, it will take more than the extension of civil partnerships for real change to take place.

One possibility would be granting cohabitants automatic rights. In 2006, Scotland introduced a set of limited rights for cohabitants who separate, or in cases where one partner dies.[2] While the Civil Partnerships Bill had its second reading in the House of Lords last week, there are currently no plans for the second reading of the Cohabitation Rights Bill, so there's little sign of progress on that front.

But while legislation may be an important part of addressing this problem, wider societal structures, cultural norms and public attitudes are equally important. The public as a whole need to have a better understanding of their legal status, empowering them to take decisions that suit their family's circumstances. And for that, a combined effort will be needed: one involving government, lawyers, practitioners, wider society – and, I hope – social researchers.

22 January 2019

Footnotes
1. https://www.ons.gov.uk/peoplepopulationandcommunity/ birthsdeathsandmarriages/families/bulletins/familiesandhouseholds/2017

2. Under the Family Law (Scotland) Act 2006, which came into force in May 2006, cohabitants (opposite-sex and same-sex couples) may make limited claims against each other in the event of their relationship terminating or on the death of one cohabitant

Healthy living with long-time partner

Several studies have found that marriage has health benefits, but new research shows that living in a partnership – married or not – is good for your health. Couples living together in long-term relationships seem to be as healthy as married couples, according to a study led by Dr Brienna Perelli-Harris at the ESRC Centre for Population Change.

The study compared data from five countries: the US, UK, Australia, Germany and Norway. The findings indicate that there is a consistent, positive association between living in a partnership and health in middle age across all countries.

Partnerships seem to be important for both men and women's health, but other aspects of people's lives contribute to how they rate their health – and whether they feel that they benefit from living with a partner.

Earlier research suggests that in the UK and US, living together without being married is associated with disadvantage and poverty. Welfare policies can also strengthen this trend; low benefits coupled with low income can make it more difficult for individuals to become sufficiently secure financially to feel they are in a position to marry.

In contrast to the US and UK, respondents in Australia, Norway, and Germany rate their health at similar levels regardless of whether they are cohabiting or married in middle age. In Australia there is a legal recognition of cohabiting partnerships which likely follows a general social acceptance where fewer people feel the need to marry. Norway has a long history of cohabitation without any current stigma attached, and is moving towards legally equalising cohabitation and marriage.

'Significant differences between cohabitation and marriage are only evident in the US and the UK; however, they disappear when economic background is taken into account,' the researchers state in a concluding paragraph. 'The findings suggest that cohabitation in the US and UK, both liberal welfare regimes, seems to be very different than in the other countries. The results challenge the assumption that only marriage is beneficial for health.'

22 February 2019

www.esrc.ukri.org

CAN YOU SPOT THE DIFFERENCE?

MARRIED

LONG TERM PARTNERSHIP

Answer:
Trick question! Both couples have happy and healthy lifestyles.

Children's well-being and social relationships, UK: 2018

How children aged ten to 15 years in the UK are coping in a range of areas that matter to their quality of life, reflecting the circumstances of their lives and their own perspectives.

- The proportion of children aged ten to 15 years who argued more than once a week with their mother fell significantly from 30.5% in 2009 to 2010 to 25.8% in 2015 to 2016.

- The proportion of children aged ten to 15 years who talked to their father more than once a week about things that mattered to them increased significantly from 38.0% in 2009 to 2010 to 45.2% in 2015 to 2016.

- The growth in children talking to their fathers more was driven largely by girls, who reported an increase from 35.7% in 2009 to 2010 to 45.6% in 2015 to 2016, making this aspect of children's relationships with their fathers now very similar for both boys and girls.

- The proportion of children aged ten to 15 years reporting high or very high happiness with friends fell significantly from 85.8% in 2015 to 80.5% in 2017, with boys being the main driver of this change.

- The proportion of children aged ten to 15 years who reported using social networking sites for more than three hours on a normal school day increased significantly from 8.6% in 2010 to 2011 to 12.8% in 2015 to 2016, with girls more than twice as likely to spend this length of time using social networking sites.

The importance of relationships to children's well-being

Children's well-being is an important part of the nation's well-being. Not only does childhood set the foundation for a well-functioning and healthy adulthood, but children ought to be able to experience life and flourish as individuals.

The importance of social connections to well-being throughout our lives is something that is gaining increasing policy attention. The Prime Minister recently announced the development of a strategy to alleviate loneliness in response to the Jo Cox Commission, and requested the Office for National Statistics (ONS) to develop measures of loneliness for use with people of all ages. As this is such an important issue, children's family and social relationships are the focus of this article as part of the latest update of the children's well-being indicators.

Most people experience loneliness at some point during their lifetime. For children, one of the first reasons for loneliness is an absence of peer friendship, with an increasing focus on quality of friendships rather than quantity as children move into late childhood and adolescence.

In March 2017, the government laid an amendment to the Children and Social Work Act 2017 by making Relationships Education statutory in all schools. The focus will be on different types of relationships, how to recognise, understand and build healthy relationships, how relationships may affect health and well-being, including

mental health, as well as healthy relationships and safety online. In subsequent sections, this article will cover a range of issues relating to children's social, family and community relationships using the data collected and analysed as part of the children's well-being indicators.

Family relationships

In *The Good Childhood Report 2013*, The Children's Society found that a measure of family harmony was substantially more indicative of children's well-being than family structure. Additionally, they also found that the quality of family relationships was one of the three most significant aspects of life that contributes to children's overall sense of well-being.

Talking to parents

The percentage of children in the UK who reported talking to their father more than once a week about things that matter to them increased significantly between 2009 to 2010 and 2015 to 2016, increasing from 38.0% to 45.2%. This improvement was largely driven by girls, with 45.6% reporting regularly talking to their father in 2015 to 2016, compared with 35.7% in 2009 to 2010, making this aspect of children's relationships with their fathers now very similar for both boys and girls.

A greater percentage of children reported talking to their mother more than once a week about things that matter to them; however, this improvement was not significant. Despite this, children were significantly more likely to report talking to their mother than to their father. In 2015 to 2016, 64.9% of children reported regularly talking to their mother about things that matter, while only 45.2% of children reported regular conversations with their father in the same time period.

It is important to note that these analyses do not take family composition or living arrangements into account and specifically how these might relate to opportunities for interaction between parents and children.

Arguing with parents

Between 2009 to 2010 and 2015 to 2016, the percentage of children aged 10 to 15 years who argued with their mother more than once a week fell significantly, from 30.5% to 25.8%. Again, girls were the main driver, as the percentage of girls who reported regularly arguing with their mother in this time period also decreased significantly, falling from 31.0% to 25.2%. This marks the first time that boys have been more likely to report arguing with their mother than girls.

Despite this decrease, children remained significantly more likely to report frequent arguments with their mother than with their father. In 2015 to 2016, 25.8% of children reported arguing with their mother more than once a week, while

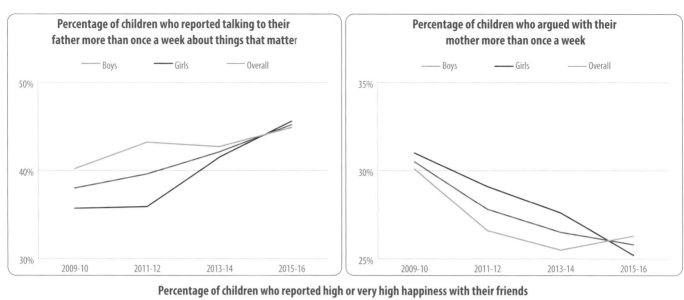

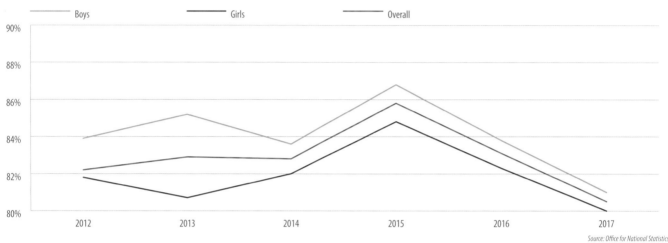

Percentage of children who reported high or very high happiness with their friends

Source: Office for National Statistics

19.2% of children reported arguing with their father more than once a week in the same time period.

Again, it is important to note that family composition or living arrangements have not been taken into account for the purposes of these analyses. There is potential for further analyses to understand how this may impact interactions between parents and children.

Relationships with friends

Relationships with friends are also important to a child's well-being. The 2013 NatCen report *Predicting Well-being* found that children with good social relationships with both family and friends were more likely to have higher well-being.

Relationships have also been examined in the wider context. In the most recent *The Good Childhood Report 2017*, The Children's Society found that there was some evidence that social media may have a beneficial association for satisfaction with friendships. However, there was also the recognition of the negative consequences of heavy social media use such as fear of missing out and potential for cyberbullying. A recent inquiry on cyberbullying conducted by The Children's Society highlighted the negative impact that online bullying can have on children and young people's mental health, with a call for social media companies to do more to tackle the issues.

Happiness with friends

Between 2015 and 2017, the percentage of children aged ten to 15 years who reported high or very high happiness with their friends fell significantly, from 85.8% to 80.5%. The drop was slightly larger for boys than girls, with the percentage of boys who reported high or very high happiness with their friends falling significantly from 86.8% to 81.0%. The percentage of girls reporting high or very high happiness with their friends also fell, from 84.8% to 80.0%.

Despite the significant changes between 2015 and 2017, it is important to be aware that the data on happiness with friends has been volatile over the five-year period and so it will be interesting to see if this pattern continues in the future or whether the data levels out again. However, evidence from other sources does suggest that children may be struggling more with social relationships. For example, ChildLine has reported an increasing number of calls from children and young people about loneliness and now have a call category specifically devoted to this to monitor the trend more closely going forward.

26 March 2018

Children's wellbeing not negatively affected by living in single parent households, study shows

The experience of single parenthood is more common than typically reported – and children's wellbeing is not negatively affected by living in single parent households – according to a study led by the University of Sheffield.

A report by Sumi Rabindrakumar, in her role as policy officer at the leading national charity working with single parent families, Gingerbread, and University of Sheffield researchers, found that public policy and research needs a more nuanced understanding of single parent family life – reflecting how households change over time.

The study, carried out as part of the University's Crook Public Service Fellowship scheme, explored the experiences of more than 27,800 households with children over a six-year period.

It found that, while surveys typically suggest that one in four families with children are headed by a single parent at any one point in time, data suggests that one in three families with children will have been a single parent family at some point over a six-year period.

Rosie Ferguson, Chief Executive at Gingerbread, said: 'We have been supporting single parent families for a hundred years and we know first-hand how strong and diverse single parents and their families are.

'Our report with the University of Sheffield debunks myths about single parent households and significantly, it shows that children are not negatively impacted if raised by a lone parent. What is most important to a child's wellbeing is the presence of positive relationships.

'We urge policy-makers and researchers alike to do more to challenge popular stereotypes and reflect the dynamism of family life.'

The report found transitions out of single parent family status are also common. Over six years, one in seven single parents reported getting married or cohabiting – and of these parents, nearly three-quarters re-partnered with a biological parent of their child.

The study also found there is no evidence of a negative impact of living in a single parent household on children's wellbeing in terms of their self-reported life satisfaction, quality of peer relationships, or positivity about family life. Children who are living or have lived in single parent families score as highly – or higher – against each measure of wellbeing as those who have always lived in two parent families.

Sumi Rabindrakumar, report author, added: 'By taking a more dynamic view of family life, these findings challenge common political and public narratives around single parents and their families.

'Not only is the experience of single parenthood more common than typically reported, but family and caring relationships are more complex and often extend beyond the household unit.

'Crucially, there are clear signs that children's wellbeing is not negatively affected by living within a single parent household. This fresh look at family life must now be reflected in policy making and research alike. To ignore these trends risks remaining out of touch with the reality of everyday lives and the UK's family landscape.'

The study found that policy-makers should recognise the fluidity of families and separation – single parenthood is common and separation in itself does not mean the breakdown of relationships with a child's biological parent, particularly given the prevalence of re-partnering for biological parents.

They should also think beyond the household and understand and value the support networks and relationships between and within households in policy decisions.

Policy-makers should also resist popular narratives regarding the perceived 'problems' of single parenthood for children and ensure targeted policy making by taking proper account of the evidence on what affects family outcomes.

Professor Nathan Hughes, from the University of Sheffield's Department of Sociological Studies, said: 'These findings have clear implications for how single parent families should be understood, valued and supported. Stereotyping single parenthood as a problem is inaccurate and immoral.

'The evidence on what affects child and family outcomes is readily available to politicians, but often does not seem to penetrate predetermined negative political narratives about single parents.

'We need to recognise that family extends beyond the household unit. In particular, it is clear that grandparents play a key role in providing both financial and practical support, and therefore in ensuring a child's wellbeing.'

The research was carried out by a multidisciplinary team as part of the Crook Public Service Fellowship scheme in the University of Sheffield's Faculty of Social Sciences.

The Crook Public Service Fellowship scheme, named in honour of the donor, Emeritus Professor Tony Crook, CBE FAcSS FRTPI, from the University of Sheffield's Department of Urban Studies and Planning and former Pro-Vice-Chancellor, aims to encourage original thinking and influence public policy.

The initiative allows future leaders in the public and not-for-profit sector to work closely with academics on pressing policy issues to influence their sector and wider society.

Professor Crook said: 'I am delighted to see how the Crook Fellowships have achieved what I wanted to see when we set these up. They are helping to build strong collaborations between academic colleagues and Crook Fellows working in the policy and practice communities.

'The fundamental aim is to help make the world a better place through rigorous research on difficult policy challenges. These reports show what we can do through building strong links between academics and policy makers.'

27 December 2018

Fathers develop children's social skills to make friends

Dads can provide secure attachment, sensitive play and opportunities in the world that support children's social and emotional learning.

By Professor Ross D. Parke

Fathers are vital for development of children's social skills, their relationships with peers and friends, their capacities to resolve conflict and their abilities to concentrate. Dad is also an important provider of social opportunities in the outside world. He is, in short, a route to resilience and children's lifelong success at home and beyond.

These contributions to children's social skills and thinking capacities challenge policy to prepare and educate boys properly for fatherhood. They require development of public services for parents that support fathers as well as mothers. The workplace should become father-friendly, and the media's often negative depictions of fatherhood should be updated to recognise and promote paternal competence. Policy should ensure that fathers and mothers are treated equally within the law. Public policy and practice in most countries typically fails in at least some of these requirements, and sometimes in all.

Developing social skills

The role of fathers in social and emotional learning begins with infants' early attachment. Having secure attachment with fathers as well as mothers in infancy bequeaths long-term benefits in terms of social skills. It is the start of a lengthy, continuous process that leads to other patterns of interactions, notably during play.

Children's play with their fathers is no idle pastime. It is often the physical context in which children develop social skills they need to make and keep friends. It provides the guidebook for how to manage relationships.

Getting along with peers and making friends

In studies, we observed fathers who moderated their physical play to a pace that suited their children, slowing down when the child was getting overwhelmed, being sensitive to facial expressions that called for gentler play. Likewise, we observed that if a child was too unruly, dad might frown and the child slowed down. The children of these fathers – whose relationships involved mutual

regulation – were more successful with peers. They had learned how to recognise and produce the emotional cues for managing relationships well. They knew how to avoid becoming too angry or sad or flat, and how to keep their emotions at levels that were not too exhausting. This gave them resilience.

How fathers play

Our studies have also shown that successful playful interaction with fathers in first grade is related to better concentration skills in children and predicts academic achievement in third grade. Good father play is also linked to social skills such as politeness and the capacity to display a positive attitude in the face of disappointment. In short, children gain a package of social and emotional learning in their interactions with their fathers that they can apply to a variety of situations.

'The dad dance – the to-and-fro of father-child interaction in which each grows sensitive and responsive to the other – is a rhythm that children ultimately transfer to their other relationships. We should help them get the rhythm right.'

Children who are securely attached to both their mothers and fathers typically expect that the world will be a positive place and will respond to them in positive ways.

Well-adapted children typically have fathers who advise them about and exemplify how to repair relationships, solve problems and rectify past wrongs – cognitive templates for maintaining good relationships with friends and others.

Decades of work on how mothers and fathers resolve conflict also shows that after parents have a falling out, if they resolve things in a constructive way, the children will do better and be more able to manage their own emotions.

Mothers are, of course, very important for children's emotional development and managing relationships with friends. However, their contributions often take a different form. They are more likely to provide the language or vocabulary of emotion and to deliver it in a didactic/teaching format. Fathers tend more to provide their social and emotional learning in an interactional/playful context and in less linguistic form.

Supporting social and emotional learning from fathers

The question for policy makers is how to make the most of fathers' contributions to children's social skills, which come in three parts: secure attachment and social interaction; advice on problem solving for relationships with friends or peers, and showing how mum and dad resolve their conflicts; and fathers' role as monitor and provider of social opportunities.

Supporting secure attachment and good interaction means giving fathers as well as mothers a generous supply of information about parenthood. It also means equality for fathers as competent care givers in terms of time with children after divorce or separation.

The medical establishment should welcome fathers during pregnancy, in the delivery room and in the postpartum period. We filmed new fathers being instructed about how to feed and hold a baby: just 15 minutes made a difference to their parental competence three months later. Healthcare practitioners should recognise that they are supporting a family unit, not just a mother-infant pair. They should also reach out to diverse families. The programmes pioneered by Carolyn and Philip Cowan have recognised the wide range of people who need parental support. These include poorer families who might not avail themselves of a programme, people who are incarcerated and those who have previously been abusive.

The rules around adoption should be opened up so it is easier for gay or single men to adopt. In the United States, far too many children, particularly those with special needs or from ethnic minorities, remain in institutional care, when there are eligible men available to parent them and give them the start in life that they need.

Thinking afresh about fathers

Governments must recognise that fathers are more than a paycheque. Evidence demonstrates that they can provide much more that is vital to child development than simply their financial contribution. Yet, in many countries, mothers on welfare are financially penalised if they have a cohabiting man in the household, on the assumption that these men are providing financial support. Often, however, a man may provide little income, but may help to stabilise a mother's relationship with her children. In discouraging cohabitation, the state may be depriving children of the stimulation, teaching and social skills support that he can bring.

Family-workplace policies are a major issue. Rather than maternal or paternal leave, we need family leave, which reconceptualises child rearing as a shared enterprise and creates the flexibility for couples to negotiate who takes leave entitlements. This step is just one part of rethinking the workplace so that men have genuine access to benefits such as job shares, flexi-time and part-time work that have long been more easily available to women.

Making life better for fathering begins at school. The segregation of roles for men and women is coming to an end at work and at home. So, for example, there is a welcome and positive focus in schools, galvanised at the level of the United Nations, to prepare girls for careers in STEM – science, technology, engineering and maths. But we have not begun to prepare boys in schools for the new space that is opening up to them as caring fathers. We need to educate both boys and girls for a world in which boys don't have to follow a patriarchal script. They can follow a more egalitarian script and still be masculine.

It's time to stop underestimating and undermining fathers to the detriment of their children's development and their social skills. The dad dance – the to-and-fro of father-child interaction in which each grows sensitive and responsive to the other – is a rhythm that children ultimately transfer to relationships with friends, peers and the adult world. We should do everything we can to help them get the rhythm right.

July 2018

www.childandfamilyblog.com

Identified: the families with the most sibling bullying

- Sibling bullying does have an impact on mental health later in life, and parents and health professionals need to take it seriously to prevent it.

- There are characteristics in families that make sibling bullying more likely.

- Family constellation and early experiences predict families with more sibling bullying.

Sibling bullying does have an effect on mental health later in life for both the victims and the bullies, it needs to be taken more seriously by parents and healthcare professionals. There are families where sibling bullying is more likely and can be prevented – say researchers in the Department of Psychology at the University of Warwick.

Prof. Dieter Wolke and PhD student Slava Dantchev have previously found that sibling bullying does have an effect on mental health later on in life in previous research but now they have identified the factors in a family that sibling bullying is more likely to occur in their paper *Trouble in the Nest: Antecedents of Sibling Bullying Victimization and Perpetration* published in *Developmental Psychology* 14 February 2019.

Using the Avon Longitudinal Study of Parents and Children (ALSPAC, also known as the Children of the 90s study), they identified factors in families that may predict sibling bullying, as the victim and the perpetrator.

The factors fell into four categories:

1. Structural family characteristics – e.g. birth order, number of children in the household, number of older brothers/sisters, marital status in the family, education level and financial difficulties.

2. Parental and parenting characteristics – e.g. postnatal mental health, maternal bonding, conflicting partnerships or domestic violence.

3. Early social experiences – e.g time spent with siblings, aggression between them and peer bullying

4. Individual differences – e.g. gender of child, child temperament and IQ

There were three different types of bullying monitored – Physical, psychological and social.

The researchers analysed data from 6,838 British children born in either 1991 or 1992. 28.1% of them were involved in any kind of sibling bullying.

Psychological bullying was the most reported type of bullying, and males bullied their siblings more often than females.

Those who most often perpetrated bullying against siblings were first-born children, those growing up in families with more children at home, who had parents who did not effectively parent or themselves had conflicts with each other and the children showed early-on aggressive tendencies.

Most interesting, whether the family experienced financial difficulties, came from a higher or lower social class, two or single parent household or whether mothers had higher or lower levels of education did not predict sibling bullying.

Findings suggest sibling bullying is an evolutionary driven strategy towards maintaining or achieving social dominance, and older siblings are at particular risk of initiating sibling bullying.

Prof. Wolke and Slava say parents may benefit from education about how to deal with resource losses for first-borns, and how to manage them in fostering improved sibling relationships. Interventions that may help both parents and children reduce aggression and bullying might be useful for affected families.

Prof. Dieter Wolke of the Department of Psychology at the University of Warwick comments:

'This is the first study that has looked at risk factors for sibling bullying from pregnancy to early adolescence. Sibling aggression is driven by loss of resources for firstborns and later born defending their need for resources such as parent attention or material goods. Sibling bullying has a class blindness: it is as much an issue in well-to-do families as those who are financially just getting by.'

First author Slava Dantchev adds:

'This and our previous findings of the adverse effects of sibling bullying on mental health make it clear that parents may benefit from information on how to identify and deal with sibling bullying.'

14 February 2019

www.warwick.ac.uk

What will British families be arguing about this Christmas?

Young people and families with kids are most likely to think things will get tense around the Christmas tree. But what is everyone bickering about?

By Victoria Waldersee

Christmas might be a wonderful chance to catch up with family... but it can also get tense. One in three Brits (29%) think it's likely they'll have an argument with their family at some point during Christmas.

Those aged 18 to 24 – the demographic most likely to be spending the holidays with their parents (77%) – are significantly more likely to predict a fight. One in five of this group (22%) say a row is 'very likely', and another one in four (26%) think it's 'fairly likely'. Just one in ten of them (10%) think it's 'not at all likely' that things will kick off, compared to almost a third (28%) of the population as a whole.

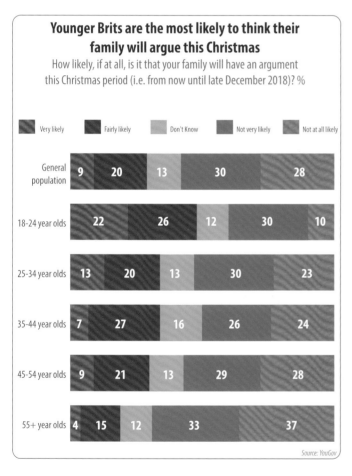

Younger Brits are the most likely to think their family will argue this Christmas

How likely, if at all, is it that your family will have an argument this Christmas period (i.e. from now until late December 2018)? %

Legend: Very likely | Fairly likely | Don't Know | Not very likely | Not at all likely

	Very likely	Fairly likely	Don't Know	Not very likely	Not at all likely
General population	9	20	13	30	28
18-24 year olds	22	26	12	30	10
25-34 year olds	13	20	13	30	23
35-44 year olds	7	27	16	26	24
45-54 year olds	9	21	13	29	28
55+ year olds	4	15	12	33	37

Source: YouGov

The presence of children in the house makes an argument 40% more likely: 38% with a child in the house foresee a Christmas row, compared to 26% of those in childless households.

What are we all bickering about?

The most likely trigger for an argument at the dinner table this Christmas is, quite simply, 'family stuff'. In other words, long-standing family tensions (37%) and sibling rivalries (22%).

In a similar vein, one in five (18%) fear their families' sportsmanship levels will be lacking: games and family activities are likely to kick off a fight, they say.

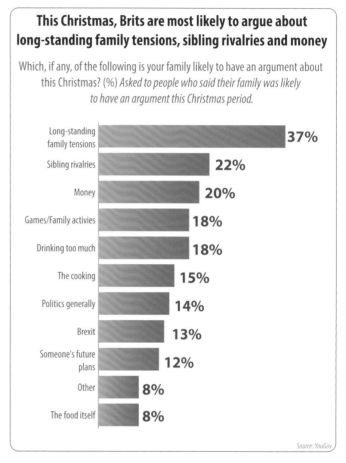

This Christmas, Brits are most likely to argue about long-standing family tensions, sibling rivalries and money

Which, if any, of the following is your family likely to have an argument about this Christmas? (%) *Asked to people who said their family was likely to have an argument this Christmas period.*

Long-standing family tensions	37%
Sibling rivalries	22%
Money	20%
Games/Family activies	18%
Drinking too much	18%
The cooking	15%
Politics generally	14%
Brexit	13%
Someone's future plans	12%
Other	8%
The food itself	8%

Source: YouGov

One in eight Brits will be bickering over Brexit (13%) or politics more broadly (14%).

Even food will cause tension, with one in six (15%) thinking there'll be fights over the cooking, and one in twelve (8%) arguing over the food itself (such as how much everyone gets). One in five (18%) think a row will emerge about how much someone is drinking.

According to the Omnibus survey, men are almost twice as likely as women to think money, or someone's future plans, will cause a fight (27% vs 14%, and 15% vs 9%). Those aged 18 to 24 are also more likely than average to think money will be a source of tension (27% vs 20% of the population as a whole).

18 December 2018

Young people who frequently argue with their parents are better citizens, research finds

Teenagers who regularly clash with their parents are more likely to have given time to a charity or humanitarian cause, a study has shown.

The survey of 13- and 14-year-olds carried out by academics at Cardiff University, showed those who argued 'a lot' with their mother and father, compared to those who 'never' argued, were also more likely to have been involved with a human rights organisation in the past 12 months and to have contacted a politician or signed a petition.

Professor Sally Power, of the Wales Institute of Social & Economic Research, Data & Methods (WISERD), who led on the study, said: 'Traditionally, rows between teenagers and their parents have been seen as an unwelcome and stressful part of growing up.

'In actual fact, our research indicates arguments may be one route through which young people acquire skills of debate that enable them to have higher levels of civic engagement.'

The research also revealed:

◆ Girls are nearly twice as likely to have arguments with both their mother and father over their clothes;

◆ Girls are more likely to have arguments with their mother over household chores;

◆ Boys were twice as likely to argue with their mothers (but not their fathers) about politics;

◆ Boys were also more likely to have arguments with their mothers over homework.

When focusing on the ethnicity of respondents, the research revealed white teenagers were more likely than those from BAME backgrounds to argue about chores and money. The analysis also showed BAME (black, Asian and minority ethnic) respondents were seven times more likely to argue about religion.

Mothers were more likely to argue with their children than fathers, according to the survey. Nearly 83% of teenagers questioned said they never argued with grandparents.

Professor Power said: 'Our research reveals some interesting discrepancies between males and females, as well as a difference between white and BAME families. We need to delve deeper to investigate why this is the case and what effect it has on children as they grow.'

20 July 2018

Friends, frenemies and fakers

Friendships make us happier people. Friends can support us when life gets tough and celebrate with us when we've achieved something. They come in many shapes and sizes; every friend can bring something different and exciting to our lives. Good friends are funny, caring and kind and you probably see them most days at school, clubs or in your neighbourhood.

We also hang out with friends online. A Facebook friend may show love on your photos, or a gaming friend may challenge you to a game on *Roblox*. But the Internet has changed the definition of a friend – now, friends aren't necessarily people you know and see 'in real life', they can also be people who you only know online. When you're getting to know someone online, and you can't always see their facial expressions or hear the sound of their laugh, it might not be as easy to tell if they're being genuine. Remember – it's easy for people to 'catfish' you by pretending to be someone else online. Find out how to spot the fakers here.

The online and real life chats that we have with friends, family or even boyfriends and girlfriends can make us feel loved and special. You're more likely to trust your friends with things that you don't tell everyone, like your personal information or something you've never told anyone before. Whether your friends are online or in real life, it's important to make sure they're good friends… and not frenemies!

What makes a good friend?

Good friends make you feel…

- Valued and accepted
- Listened to
- Respected
- Happy and safe.

Bad friends make you feel…

- That you're not good enough
- Pressured into doing things
- Like your opinion doesn't matter
- Judged for your decisions.

Frenemies

Sometimes friendships are not healthy.

Five signs that you've got a frenemy

1. Your friend is jealous when you talk to other friends, or if you achieve something, they aren't happy for you.
2. Your friend calls you nasty names, or says mean things about your appearance either online or in real life.
3. Your friend pressures you into doing something that you don't want to do. They might share images of you without your permission.
4. Your friend tries to monitor and control you, perhaps by checking your phone or telling you who you can and can't follow on social media.
5. Your friend says bad things will happen to you if you don't do what they want. They might get annoyed if you don't respond to their messages as quickly as they would like.

Dealing with frenemies

Don't share personal information with someone you don't trust

Don't tell someone that you don't trust any of your personal information, or things that you keep private. They could share this information with others that you wouldn't want to tell.

Trust your instincts

If you feel sad after you speak to a certain friend, and you don't think they're treating you right, trust yourself and speak to an adult.

Don't ever think it's your fault

If someone is controlling, hurting or pressuring you, it's never your fault and there is always someone who can help.

Speak to Childline or The Mix

You can post messages and get advice on Childline's Message boards or if you want to speak to someone confidentially you can call Childline on 0800 1111. Alternatively, The Mix have a crisis messenger text service which provides 24/7 support across the UK. If a friend is causing you painful emotions, you can text THEMIX to 85258.

Speak to CEOP

If a friend is pressuring you to do something sexual that you don't want to do, talk to an adult you trust or report to CEOP. Whatever may have happened CEOP will understand. You won't be in trouble.

The above information is reprinted with kind permission from Thinkuknow.
© Crown copyright 2019

www.thinkuknow.co.uk

How imaginary friends from our childhood can continue to affect us as adults

An article from The Conversation.

THE CONVERSATION

By Paige Davis, Lecturer in Psychology, York St John University

Crabby crab is my four-year-old son Fisher's imaginary friend. Crabby appeared on a holiday in Norway by scuttling out of his ear after a night of tears from an earache. Like other childhood imaginary friends, Crabby should be an indication that Fisher's mind is growing and developing positively. Indeed, research shows that invisible companions can help boost children's social skills.

But what happens when children grow up and their imaginary friends disappear? Will Crabby have influenced Fisher into adolescence or adulthood? And what if you continue to have imaginary friends as an adult? The vast majority of the research on imaginary friends looks at young children as this is the time when these playmates are most likely to appear. But researchers have started looking into the impact of imaginary childhood friends in adolescence and adulthood.

Imaginary friends in childhood are classified as invisible beings that a child gives a mind or personality to and plays with for over three months.

It is very rare that adults have imaginary companions. But there are a few different types of behaviour that could be considered a form of imaginary friendship. For example, adult authors can be seen as prolific creators of imaginary friends in the form of characters. That's because their characters have personalities and minds of their own, and authors often report their characters leading the writing rather than vice versa. Tulpas, objects created through spiritual or mental powers in mysticism, are also a sort of imaginary friend.

Social skills in adolescence

Research has shown that the positive effects of having imaginary friends as a child continue into adulthood. Adolescents who remember their imaginary playmates have been found to use more active coping styles, such as seeking advice from loved ones rather than bottling things up inside, like their peers. Even adolescents with behavioural problems who had imaginary friends as children have been found to have better coping skills and more positive adjustment through the teenage years.

Scientists think this could be because these teens have been able to supplement their social world with imagination rather than choosing to be involved in relationships with more difficult classmates. It could also be because the imaginary friends help to alleviate these adolescents' loneliness.

These teens are also more likely to seek out social connections. Some older research suggests that such adolescents have higher levels of psychological distress than their peers who do not remember having imaginary playmates. But the majority of research being done points to mainly positive outcomes. Current research being done now by my student, Tori Watson, is taking this evidence and looking at how adolescents who report having imaginary friends as children deal with bullying at school. We suspect that teens who remember their imaginary friends will be better at dealing with bullying.

Creativity and hallucinations

Adults who had imaginary friends, meanwhile, report that they are more creative and imaginative than those who did not. We also know that they are better at describing a scene that they have constructed in their imagination. This could be because they were more imaginative to start with and/or that playing with an imaginary friend in childhood helped boost such capabilities.

There are also other discrepancies in how adults see and interact with the world around them that scientists think stems from the use of imagination when playing with an invisible friend as a child. For example, adults who had imaginary friends talk to themselves more. This is thought to be because they have grown up being more comfortable talking when no one else real is around. Interestingly, research has shown that talking to yourself can be a sign of high cognitive functioning and creativity.

Adults who had imaginary companions as children may become used to seeing things that aren't really there and explaining them to people. For this reason, imaginary friends have been looked at as a type of hallucination that is experienced by normally developing children. Importantly, the children know that these friends aren't actually real. Adults similarly can have hallucination experiences when going in or coming out of a deep sleep. We sometimes also see or hear things that aren't there, for example in the corner of our eye – knowing it's our mind playing tricks on us.

My team and I recently investigated whether people who had imaginary friends as children also report more such hallucination experiences. Interestingly, our study, published in *Psychiatry Research*, found that this actually is the case. Importantly, these individuals were not at greater risk of developing psychosis or schizophrenia, they were just more likely to have common forms of hallucinations. We know that because we also tested other perceptual experiences like unusual thoughts and ideas as well as symptoms of depression. These experiences, in combination with more intense hallucinations, can put people at higher risk of developing schizophrenia.

But people who had had imaginary friends didn't show this combination of symptoms. There was one exception, though – individuals who had also suffered child abuse. These people were more likely to have both unusual thoughts and ideas, and depression, possibly making them more vulnerable to psychosis. It's unclear whether this link has got anything to do with imaginary friends or whether it is all down to the trauma of having suffered child abuse, with imaginary friends instead playing a comforting role.

So while we know a lot about childhood imaginary friends such as Crabby Crab, and the positive effects they can have, there is still a lot to learn about imaginary friends and how our childhood experiences with them might make us see the world differently.

8 March 2019

This is how many hours it takes to become best friends, according to new study

It's not as simple as you think

By Olivia Petter

Notting Hill fans will recall a pivotal moment when Julia Roberts' character, a famous actress, is unwillingly sworn into a pact of best friendship by Hugh Grant's fan-girling sister, Honey.

However, despite shameless cajolery – 'I think you're the most beautiful woman in the world' – Honey's enthusiastic supposition that she and Roberts' character 'can be best friends' goes politely unrequited.

Evidently, when it comes to friendship, flattery will get you nowhere, so what will?

According to a new study published in the *Journal of Social and Personal Relationships*, time is everything, i.e. the longer you spend with someone, the more likely you are to develop a close bond with them – this was never going to work in Honey's favour, given she and Roberts' character had only just met when she proposed best friendship.

Author Jeffrey Hall, a communications professor at the University of Kansas, was motivated to delve into the depths of what constitutes close friendship after examining the work of evolutionary psychologist Robin Dunbar, who claimed that there are layers of friendship and limitations to how many the brain can manage.

For example, he claimed that most people classify friendships in the following categories: acquaintances, casual friends, friends, and good friends. He also theorised that the majority of us are closest to just five people and call about 15 people good friends while 150 is the estimated limit for how many relationships the brain can handle overall.

Hall conducted two separate studies to examine these layers further, specifically looking at how hours spent together correlated to closeness.

In the first study, he surveyed 355 adults who had recently moved to a new area and asked them to identify someone they had just met there who wasn't a romantic interest.

Each participant then had to reveal how they met this person, how much time they'd spent together and subsequently classify the level of friendship achieved after a longer period of time on a scale ranging from acquaintance to best friend.

For the next study, Hall asked 112 first-year students at the University of Kansas to name two new people they'd met and surveyed them for a nine-week period to see how these relationships developed.

After careful analysis, Hall found that it took roughly 200 hours to achieve best-friend status while it took 50 hours to move from acquaintances to casual friends and 90 hours to progress from casual friends to friends.

However, he added that this doesn't necessarily mean you are guaranteed to become best friends with someone if you spend 200 hours with them – it's the quality of time spent together that is crucial.

'When you spend time joking around, having meaningful conversations, catching up with one another, all of these types of communication episodes contribute to speedier friendship development,' Hall told *Psychology Today*.

Asking questions about that person's day, for example, is one way to achieve this.

The opposite effect can be seen between colleagues, who might have spent well over the 200-hour threshold together and remain acquaintances.

'You wander into the office and you say, "Hey" That's it,' he said, explaining that this very basic level of interaction will rarely lead to close friendship, regardless of hours spent together. This might be because you simply don't like this person.

So, the secret to forming long-lasting friendships might not be Honey-style flattery, nor is it a case of simply lingering in the presence of said desired friend-to-be for hours on end.

'You have to invest,' Hall concludes.

'It's clear that many adults don't feel they have a lot of time, but these relationships are not going to develop just by wanting them. You have to prioritise time with people.'

6 April 2018

Social media updates 'killing conversations' between friends

Majority of Britons say talking "in real life" no longer needed thanks to platforms such as Facebook, Twitter and Instagram.

By Paul Gallagher

Social media updates are killing conversations between friends with the majority of Britons saying they no longer need to talk face to face.

Some 51 per cent of the public say chatting to friends 'in real life' is unnecessary because they are kept up to date on what people are up to via platforms such as Facebook, Instagram and Twitter.

A poll of 5,000 adults across the UK by the mental health campaign group Time to Change also found the average person has 770 friends on social media, yet nearly a fifth (18 per cent) of us say we would not feel able to call upon any of those friends if we were struggling with our mental health.

While social media allows people to connect with those around them and can be a helpful source of support for the one in four who experience mental health problems in any given year, according to campaigners, the new data suggests 'surface level' engagement, such as liking photos or checking friends' profiles is replacing more meaningful conversation, both on and offline.

The figures, released on Time to Talk Day, reveal the impact of social media on conversation. The event, now in its sixth year, is run by Time to Change in partnership with See Me Scotland, Change Your Mind Northern Ireland and Time to Change Wales.

'Rich and busy'

Emily, a 28-year-old social media influencer, said she was guilty of having far fewer conversations. 'My friends are less likely to reach out to me to make plans because they interpret my life as being very full and rich and busy when they look at my Instagram feed, when in reality I'm struggling,' she said.

'I'm a very active social media user because I'm an influencer and also run corporate social accounts for a living so I can definitely relate to vicariously experiencing a relationship through digital means. I'm pretty guilty of being the one that doesn't reach out because I already know what the other person is up to and feel they know I'm present for them when I like or comment on an image they've just posted on Instagram.'

Jo Loughran, director of Time to Change, which is run by charities Mind and Rethink Mental Illness, said: 'We might think we know how our friends are doing because we've seen their latest post on social media. However, in a world where many of us only share our 'best bits' online we're urging everyone to use Time to Talk Day as an opportunity to break down barriers and have real and meaningful conversations about their mental health.'

The new figures come a week after research by Cancer Research UK found those aged 18 to 24 are around 20 times more likely to never speak to their neighbours, than those aged 55 and over.

7 February 2019

Losing my best friend hurt more than any relationship break-up

By Annabel Fenwick Elliott

Almost exactly a year ago, I lost my best friend. Not to death, thank goodness, or even betrayal. In the end, I lost her to apathy – 'a lack of interest, enthusiasm, or concern', as defined by the dictionary – which ranks below death and arguably above betrayal when it comes to the sadness of a break–up.

'Break–up' is a term generally reserved to describe the dissolution of a romantic relationship, but friendship has much in common. The only thing, really, that distinguishes a lover from a friend is sex. Everything else – loyalty, support, humour and companionship – exists in both. When you break–up with a lover, the part you cry over is rarely the sex. It's the partnership you miss.

Nearly half of women in the UK admit they never take time to celebrate their female friendships, according to a recent survey. What constitutes as 'celebration' is of course highly subjective – and many women marking 'Galentine's' with their female pals today will have found their own way to define it – but I do think it highlights an important fact. That a lot of women neglect their friendships in favour of romantic relationships, and will readily admit it; not realising that with a bit of effort, they could have had both.

Comedian Jo Brand was asked, during an interview for the Made of Human podcast, for the one piece of advice she would give her younger self today, and her reply stuck with me: 'Work very hard on your friendships,' she said, 'because in the long run, they are what really count. Give them a bit of slack if they're annoying, because everyone's friends are annoying now and then. It's like watering plants. Try not to let them wither.'

If you had told Claire and I, a decade ago, that we would eventually wither, we would have laughed. It was unthinkable. Our paths crossed on day one of our first year at university in 2006, unpacking boxes in opposite rooms on the same corridor. Having briefly surveyed me, her mother turned to her and whispered: 'You two are going to be friends.'

She was right. We humans tend to choose our best friends in much the same way as our spouses – plucked from a sea of other options; the one we like most. Claire and I were each others' chosen humans. I had a wonderful boyfriend at the time, Alex, and she had one, too. Throughout university, we would all remain, for the most part, a happy family.

After graduation, both boyfriends fell away, and Claire and I moved to London to start our grown–up lives.

As we meandered through our twenties, thick as thieves, through scary jobs and grotty flats; sick pets and milestone birthdays; mad flings and shoestring travels, Claire and I collected all manner of things. Some you can stick on a mantlepiece – the cards, the photos, the funny fridge magnets – and most you can't: the in–jokes, the tears, the tiny secrets and confessions.

Our friendship was never something we took for granted. We understood it was rare and we nurtured it. I knew exactly what to say when she was sad, nervous, confused or irrational – lines from a script we'd finessed over time. She knew when I was about to do something stupid or clever even before I did, and would be ready with flowers to console or congratulate as necessary. I used to feel sorry for anyone who didn't have a Claire.

Our earnest plan, back then, was to meet the man of our dreams at around the same time (ideally they'd be brothers, or at the very least good friends), buy houses on the same street, get married a few months apart, get pregnant in perfect synchrony, send our children to the same schools, do the ironing together on Sundays, then at the end – when our offspring had fled and both our husbands had shuffled off the mortal coil – we'd eke out the rest of our days in matching rocking chairs, cackling and tearing through wine until we joined them.

Quite aside from the fact that I loathe ironing and don't particularly see the point in marriage, this plan was never going to manifest. In the same year that Claire met the man of her dreams, I moved to New York to become a travel writer. While she was busy putting down roots, I was hopping from country to country. Both of us were half–mad with glee, different though our lives had become, and our friendship was strong as ever.

Until it wasn't.

As with any relationship, the events leading to its demise felt scattered at the time – minor, odd; irrelevant, few and far between. Looking back, you could plot them on a road map to Doomsville.

There were birthday cards that got lost in the post, missed calls left unreturned, plans cancelled in ever-increasing frequency. I didn't want to attribute it to her boyfriend, who I liked very much, because surely she was better than that? We'd both had boyfriends in the past without this happening.

When she got engaged, on a hillside in Devon, I was the first friend she phoned. I whooped, I rejoiced with her, then I hung up the phone, sank into the sofa and cried.

I'd heard someone say once that weddings are like funerals for friendships, and I was adamant to prove them wrong. Still, when I met Claire to toast her engagement, I fluffed my lines. I said the wrong thing about her ring, she later told me, in agreeing with her on a something when I wasn't supposed to. Such basic chatter, but it felt like the script had changed while I wasn't looking and this new one might as well have been in Russian.

I had been writing my maid of honour speech for her since our days at university – it was one of things we often joked about. I'd already started putting anecdotes to paper when she mentioned, with a casual apathy that floored me: 'I'm

Five steps to recover your friendship

1 Stop pre-empting: Sometimes we are anxious when we don't need to be and create conflicts with friends in our heads. Your friend may be sitting thinking the same thing, or not think anything is wrong.

2 Don't be consumed by guilt: Often you feel guilty or embarrassed you haven't made contact for a while and this is what is getting in the way, try not to hold onto these feelings.

3 Face conflicts that arise: If your friendships are worthwhile you should be willing to fix them, consider what has gone wrong, what their position may be and work to a solution.

4 Set objectives: Once you've discussed the issues don't let them drag on, make a decision to move forward and set practical ways of keeping in touch and letting the other know you care.

5 Find positive aspects: Your friendship may take on a different form with distance as it can allow an escape or room to see things objectively. You may be able to help each other more so make use of the distance when you can.

Source: The Telegraph

not having a maid of honour. It's American. None of my other married friends had one.'

It was such a deeply un–Claire thing to say, so at–odds with everything she stood for, that I should have just taken my cue and exited stage left then and there. Instead, I threw her hen party, doused her bridal suite with confetti, filmed her wedding video, then hid around the corner and sobbed unhappy tears at midnight.

We still talked most days, but I was by now (unhelpfully) keeping a mental tally of her digressions, as if it were some sort of sport – half upset and half rejoicing every time she followed through on a predicted slight. I suppose I was searching for something, anything, to take away from this, and being right was the only consolation prize. Being angry, with good reason, can be so much easier than being in the wrong, and sad.

Several months later came the final blow. Alex, my university boyfriend, died of brain cancer at the age of 30, and it knocked me sideways. An invitation to his memorial came in the post, and I asked Claire to come with me. We would meet for drinks first, so went our plan, and talk about the happy years we spent with him, the jokes, the long nights, the songs.

When the day finally came, she cancelled drinks, booked a last–minute meeting at her office – not an urgent one, but the timing made sense, she explained – and said she'd meet me at the service instead.

Just as the ceremony started, Claire clattered in and spotted me. As Alex's favourite songs filled the cloisters, and the air grew thick with mourning, she grasped my hand and we cried silently, side–by–side.

It was our last moment of solidarity, and our friendship died in that church. Claire knew in her heart of hearts that I'd been too needy that day, too dramatic; an unreasonable drain on her resources. I knew with every fibre of my being that she'd been unkind, apathetic – and for the last time. We were both right. Perhaps, we were both wrong. Either way, we were strangers now.

At first, as can often be case with break-ups, the severance was a relief. Over time, my feelings moved back and forth along that well–worn spectrum of sadness and indifference. I took off the bracelet she'd had engraved for my 30th, removed a framed photo of us from the mantelpiece, carefully peeled from the wall the loving notes she'd written me in the years before she'd stopped doing that, and put them all in the attic, in the box with my old journals, tatty gig tickets and the programme from Alex's memorial.

I deleted her from Instagram, Facebook, even her number from my phone. I bid farewell to more than a decade of jokes only we were in on; and to a very niche genre of music that will forever trigger laughter wherever we might we hear it – only now we'll be laughing separately.

The dent she has left on my everyday life is palpable, but I'm used to it. The dent we left on each others' past is indelible. Flicking through the photo albums that chart most of my adulthood, once a cheering thing to do on a rainy day, will always sit a little heavy on me now. She's in all of them. Claire will forever be the person who threw my 21st birthday, and I hers. There's no erasing her from photos of my 30th, nor I from her wedding shots – unless of course there's a way to airbrush out bridesmaids.

I do wonder whether our paths will ever cross in the future, and what we would say to each other. As for the present, I have good friends around me, and a happy life. Do I miss Claire? Yes. Could anyone replace her? No. For a while, when we were different people, doing different things in a different decade – it was perfect. I suspect a time will come when I look back on it with nothing but fondness.

13 February 2019

Falling out with a friend

Falling out with a friend doesn't have to be the end of your friendship!

It's a fact of life that people (of all ages and in all walks of life) fall out! Sometimes you make up, sometimes you don't. Friends can come and go out of our lives. This is your chance to work out how you will cope with what can be really upsetting situations.

It helps to talk to someone if you're feeling down. Don't feel bad about yourself, concentrate on things you enjoy, and don't bottle things up.

Falling out with a friend

People of all ages fall out for a number of reasons. Most people will make up, but some might not. If you value the friendship then it is worth trying to make up with the person.

When the argument has settled down, try talking to them and figuring out why you are both annoyed with each other.

Compromising with each other is key to making up. You have probably said some horrible things to each other and are both at fault, but you must get over this to move on.

How can I fix it?

There's no magic cure for arguments between friends, but there are a bunch of things you can try:

Try and imagine it from the other side

When we argue, we're usually blinded by our own view of things. How would you feel if the situation were reversed? Would you see things the same way as you do now?

Find a peacemaker

Ask someone who is friends with the both of you or an adult who wasn't involved to help get you talking. Don't expect them to take sides though – it won't help and isn't fair on them.

Listen

Pay careful attention to what they say. It'll help you understand why they feel the way they do and make them more likely to listen to your point of view. By listening you'll understand why they have a different viewpoint.

Tell them how you feel

This is really important to helping them understand why you feel the way you do but don't go back over what you think they did wrong – it might re-start the argument.

Tell them how you feel in a calm and non-aggressive way. Even if you are right they won't listen to you if they don't like the way they are being spoken to.

Have a laugh

Was there a funny side to what happened? Being able to laugh about it together – particularly about yourself and how you reacted – can help heal the hurt.

Accept that you might both have been right

Being able to agree to disagree is an important part of being friends in the long term. In any case, what's more important – 'winning' an argument or keeping a mate?

What to do when your friend has a different opinion from you

Whether it's politics, religion, music taste or football, we all have different views, but respecting each others' opinions is important for maintaining positive friendships.

Try to understand their view

People come from different backgrounds and are brought up to believe in different viewpoints. We are all influenced by a number of things, such as our upbringing, our culture, parental views.

Put yourself in your friends' shoes and try to ask if you'd believe the same things if you'd had the same experiences as them.

Don't be rude or arrogant

Arguments are more likely to happen, not because you have different opinions, but because of how you put them forward. Being rude and overly dismissive of your friend's opinion will only result in them getting annoyed at you.

And... don't get personal! Even if you don't agree about the issue at hand, don't resort to putting your friend down to get your point across.

Don't dwell on it

Ask yourself, is the issue really worth falling out over? If you think talking about an issue will only lead to an argument and strain your friendship, it's ok to agree to disagree, and just leave it be.

Respect their right to an opinion

Part of living in a free society like ours is that we all come from a range of cultures and backgrounds and all share different opinions.

Even if you don't agree with someone's opinion, at least agree with their right to have it, no-one should be discriminated against for their beliefs.

Remember, you aren't the only person to have an opinion, we all have them! Wouldn't it be boring if we all shared the same opinions!?

How to cope if your friendship group becomes toxic

What to do when a group of three suddenly feels more like two plus one.

By Xenia Taliotis

1. Step back to gain perspective.

When you look at anything – be that a book, or a problem – from very close range, your vision becomes blurred and you can't make out what you're looking at. Take a deep breath and assess the situation dispassionately. Are your friends really going out much more without you, or are there just as many occasions when you're doing something with one of them, or when all three of you are out together? If they are seeing more of each other, could it be because they share an interest, or do an after-school club together that's bringing them into closer contact?

2. Remember that relationships ebb and flow.

The chances are your friendship triangle will shift and rebalance in a few weeks' time, so try to not let your concerns run away with you. Be patient and calm and give the situation time to resolve itself. Accepting that friendships change is an important part of growing up.

3. Try to let your friends know that you are feeling left out.

Start by approaching the one you are closest to and talk to her face-to-face or on the phone rather than online. There's a good chance that they're not aware that they've hurt you, or that they don't realise how important it is to you to be included.

4. Think about how to modify your reaction.

Being left out from time to time is inevitable – it happens to everyone. The important thing is not to take it too much to heart. And be careful not to exacerbate the third-wheel syndrome by being standoffish, or by waiting for others to plan events that you can go along to. Take the initiative. See what's on at the cinema and invite your friends.

5. Don't sit at home stalking them on social media.

If they're out having a good time, then so should you be. Expand your friendship circle so that you have other people to socialise with. Having two best friends is great, but you shouldn't pin your whole social life on them and them alone. Socialising with other teenagers from different schools and clubs will broaden and enhance your life.

Strong teenage friendships key to good romantic relationships in adulthood

By Tom Bawden

Teenagers who have strong relationships with people of the same gender are more likely to have satisfying romantic relationships in later life, a new study finds.

Researchers have known that the quality of an adult's romantic life is closely tied to both physical and mental health in adolescence. Now, researchers have found that the friendship skills teenagers learn with their peers of the same gender were the strongest predictor of romantic satisfaction in their late 20s and beyond.

'In spite of the emphasis teens put on adolescent romantic relationships, they turn out not to be the most important predictor of future romantic success,' says Professor Joseph Allen, of the University of Virginia.

All about skills

'Instead, it's the skills learned in friendships with peers of the same gender – skills such as stability, assertiveness, intimacy, and social competence – that correspond most closely to the skills needed for success in adult romantic relationships,' he said. The study is published in *Child Development*, a journal of the Society for Research in Child Development.

Researchers interviewed and observed 165 adolescents from ages 13 to 30, living in suburban and urban areas in the southeastern United States. The group was racially, ethnically, and socioeconomically diverse. The study assessed teenagers' own reports of the quality of their social and romantic relationships, as well as those of close friends.

24 January 2019

Good friends enrich your life

Louisa Stratton recounts how both toxic and trustworthy friendships helped her grow

To me, a good friendship is when you both feel relaxed and can have a laugh as well as sharing the more difficult stuff.

It's important to take an interest in each other's points of view, encourage each other, and take the initiative to make sure your mates are okay when something painful or stressful is going on in their lives.

It's key to be aware when other people aren't treating you well and to develop a sense of what is and isn't acceptable. But it's also important to take responsibility for your mistakes and try to fix them.

An unhealthy friendship is a burden. It takes more from you than you get, makes you feel bad about yourself. People that make you unhappy, unwanted and unvalued are not true friends.

I had a friend for a very long time, and our entire friendship was draining and complicated. She was someone that I could relate to but, as time passed, her lack of empathy became more obvious.

It was only as I realised my own worth that I noticed she was slotting me into her world of self-martyrdom. She perpetuated the idea that life was hard and she was a victim, and wouldn't listen to anyone saying otherwise.

Sure we had some good times, but the only memories I have of her now are her stressing me out.

Long story short, I have realised that getting to know a person is complicated. I thought I had someone who depended on me, but I let it sit there and be toxic and it ended up hurting both of us.

'Initially, I didn't like social media. I couldn't relate to the hype. So I ended up being an almost total social outcast, and obviously that was pretty lonely. I know now that I should have taken more of the initiative, but the pressure to conform to what everyone else was doing was enough to make it feel pointless. So many people were putting too much stock in the importance of online attention.

But social media is an amazing tool, it lets us stay connected to each other no matter the distance and explore our interests further. But it's also easy to forget that it's nothing but a tool. Being on a computer can never give you what being with good friends in real life can.

There's nothing like a fun day out with friends that you can all talk about later. Maybe not every dayout will be like an epic event, but it doesn't have to be!

Good friends enrich your life. They are interested in what you have to say, back you up when something is stressing you out, and let you rely on them from time to time, as well as depending on you.

After a long period of personal hardship, my friends and I decided to take a trip for a few days. It was the first time I had been outside the city without my family, and I wasn't confident about being away from home.

But I took the chance and was reminded just how trustworthy my friends really were. They had thought of everything and were more than willing to change the plans for my needs even when I insisted they didn't have to.

We all grew closer, we had a great time and I learned how it truly felt to put my trust in others. I was able to let myself go at my own pace because of their support.

I know from many years of being awkward that just taking the initiative can be hard, but once you've done it the rest will fall into place. Get to know people, get a read on their personality, find who you want to spend time with. It's simpler than it seems!

Sure you'll make mistakes, but in the end you'll find something that was worth all your work.

4 March 2019

Should I ban my teenager from having a boyfriend?

By Victoria Lambert

First love – whether a teenage crush, unrequited adoration or a surprisingly mature partnership – is a staple of school life. It holds, for many, a vivid place in their memories.

Yet last month, Toby Belfield, the headmaster of £34,500-a-year Ruthin School in North Wales, announced in an email to parents that any student found to have a boyfriend or girlfriend would be given worse university references and even face exclusion.

This authoritarian approach – based on Belfield's belief that puppy love is a barrier to top grades – caused equal parts outrage, hilarity and disappointment. So much so that within 24 hours, the headmaster had backtracked to saying that while 'school is not the place for romantic relationships – ever' pupils would be offered the chance to 'review their current romantic situation, and ... put their education first.'

Of course, anyone who has ever been a teenager will know that Belfield is tilting at windmills. Such a ban is unlikely to deter hormonal adolescents from finding each other. 'It is what we are hard-wired to do,' explains Jane Evans, a parenting expert. 'The human race is primed to be in relationships. You can't cut that off in school.'

Helen Gilbert, 40, a mother of three young teens from Hampshire who works in PR, agrees. 'Saying no to these relationships is wrong. Children have a natural need to have or understand male/female relationships and friendships – these are their comfort zones.

'Forbidding them will have the opposite effect, making the idea of boyfriends and girlfriends more attractive. Meanwhile, all the arguments will be time distracted from studying. Why would you even bother?'

For Lauren Derrett, author of *Filter Free: Real Life Stories of Real Women*, this attitude is a reminder of the way schools have become results-driven. Mother to four children, aged five, 14, 19 and 21, and stepmother to two more teenagers, Derrett says: 'When we say the only thing that matters is results, we are closing down other options. I want my children to be rounded people. Reaching out and learning about relationships and friendships is part of their experience and formative years.'

Furthermore, says Derrett, 'There are so many positives about relationships at this age. Children can learn about themselves, their own boundaries, their likes and dislikes together. And it's an opportunity for parents to guide them on self-respect. Young love can lead to personal growth and a better understanding of who you are as you learn to trust someone to a deeper level.'

Young love can lead to personal growth and a better understanding of who you are

Noor Hibbert, a business coach, says she recalls relationships from the age of 14 onwards. 'Perhaps inevitably,' she says, 'I endured heartache, but although the drama of these relationships and subsequent break-ups were emotionally stressful at the time, they didn't affect my academic ability and I went on to achieve three good A-levels and a degree, before becoming a successful entrepreneur.'

She adds: 'I think it's important to educate our teenagers on how to navigate through those strong emotions of relationships and how to cope when they end, rather than ban teens altogether from experiencing them.

'As much as we would love to protect our children from heartbreak, relationships are an important part of emotional growth. Studies have shown that happier students lead a fulfilling life – both in and out of school.'

Evans agrees. 'I went to an all-girls convent school and so I was vulnerable around boys. Had I known what a healthy relationship was like, I believe my academic achievement would have been better than it was.'

Perhaps Belfield doesn't understand what modern relationships are like, says Gilbert. 'Banning relationships in school misses the point that they now often begin online. In the early stages they may not even mean any real time spent together. It's someone to talk to on Snapchat and may not involve any physical contact.

'There are good and bad sides to this. On the one hand, if they choose their boy- or girlfriend from among their schoolmates, some peer pressure can protect them from getting too involved.' But she points out, the online relationship has benefits, too. 'It's a bit like old-fashioned couples courting by letter. They find it easier to talk.'

So, what can help? Some schools have realised the value of specialist advice. One such is ACS Egham International School where Debbie Stanton is school counsellor. She says: 'The sex element is covered in science lessons, but I plan the lessons for PSHE [personal, social and health education], which focus on friendship and respect. We look at consent, and ask 'are you OK, are you happy?'.

'The children know they can email me and come for a chat at any time. My job is to listen and help them make their own decisions. Sometimes that might mean talking about contraception, or it might help them feel they can stand up to someone and say they are not happy. It's about respecting them.'

Most schools don't have a dedicated counsellor, but Evans says relationships can be brought in to almost any lesson. 'We can teach them some biology, some psychology,

some physiology around how the human race is wired for relationships. We can explain how to use your emotional intelligence to work out if you are with someone who is a trustworthy, good person.'

For parents, Derrett says: 'You have to listen, respect and guide your children. Bring the relationship into the open and into your home; don't leave it in the back seat of a car.

'We can help our children, talk about their options, not scare them. Then it comes down to knowing your kids and having confidence in them.'

After all, some young love grows into a mature lasting relationship. Says Evans: 'My son and his girlfriend met at school at 17. Ten years later, they are about to get married.'

11 February 2018

Your relationship

Healthy relationships are possible and you deserve to be in one!

A healthy relationship is when two people treat each other as equals, they trust each other and treat each other with respect. In a healthy relationship, people should:

- Support each other
- Listen to each other's feelings
- When they have a disagreement, talk about it
- Spend quality time together
- Encourage each other
- Take responsibility for their own actions
- Respect women and men equally

Healthy relationships look like:

Equality

Respect – listening, being non-judgemental, understanding and valuing your opinions.

Trust – respecting your right to your own opinions, friends and activities, believing in you.

Support – supporting you in your goals and ambitions, believing in you.

Safety – respecting your personal space, non-threatening behaviour, non-manipulative or intimidating behaviour.

Honesty – clear, open and truthful communication, being able to say if you're feeling scared or insecure.

Responsibility – acknowledging one's behaviours and attitudes, asking not expecting, making decisions together.

Freedom – being able to live your life free from violence, intimidation or threatening behaviour.

Negotiation & Compromise – accepting that there isn't always a 'right' way to do things, accepting change, willingness to see the other side.

Unhealthy relationships look like:

Power & control

Using intimidation – making you afraid by using looks, actions and gestures, threatening and harassing phone calls/text messages, using their physical presence to scare you.

Using isolation – controlling what you do, who you talk to and where you go, stopping you from seeing your friends and family; your mates don't like hanging around with both of you.

Blaming, denying & minimising – denying any abuse or problems, making light of the abuse, saying it was nothing, blaming you for the abuse, blaming use of drugs or alcohol for the abuse.

Sexual abuse – forcing or pressurising you to do sexual things you don't want to, constantly putting down or criticising your body.

Emotional abuse – constantly putting you down and criticising you, calling you names, dictating and controlling what you wear, making you feel bad about yourself, playing mind games, humiliating you, making you feel guilty.

Using threats – making threats to hurt you, threatening to hurt themselves if you dump them, making threats to hurt or kill your pets, threatening to destroy your things, or to spread rumours about you.

Physical abuse – hitting you, punching you, kicking you, pushing you around, blocking your way, locking you in.

Financial abuse – making you feel guilty or like you owe them for things they have brought you, stopping you from getting work, making you depend on them for money, taking your money.

What does respect feel like?

Respect is about knowing that your feelings are just as important as everyone else's and that you deserve to be treated well… by yourself as well as by other people. Being different is OK – you are a unique and special human being with feelings, needs and rights – there's no one else quite like you!

If you want to know someone better, then respect between the two of you is about honesty, trust and communication. We all have rights and responsibilities. It's important to trust your instincts, to ask for help and to speak up for yourself.

It's also important to respect other people. This isn't necessarily about admiring them, liking them or expecting them to 'earn' it. Everyone's entitled to their own feelings and points of view, even if we don't know them or agree with them. People who have respect for others don't discriminate or bully, because they understand that other people's feelings are just as important as their own.

People who respect others will always avoid harming them, in any way, because they understand that everyone has a right to wellbeing.

How can I show respect?

If you want to know someone better, then respect between the two of you is about honesty, trust and communication. This is the kind of respect that can really help a relationship work better.

- Talking together with the other person can help you understand where you're both coming from.

- Really listening properly too (not just stopping talking once in a while!) can really help to build trust and understanding.

If you can get these right, then life will be a lot easier if you come up against the more difficult times in your relationships.

YOU know it's respectful when:

- Your partner likes you just the way you are.

- They don't expect you to look, act, dress or behave a certain way.

- They care about what you want, not just what they want.

- When it comes to sex, they are willing to wait until you're both ready, and wouldn't try and make you do anything you didn't want to, for example, something they'd seen online.

- You trust each other and can confide things in each other that you both know will stay private, just between the two of you.

- You enjoy the relationship.

How can I tell if there's a lack of respect?

Sometimes, when there is a lack of respect in a relationship, one partner may abuse their power and inflict harm on the other person.

This can happen through social media; for example, your partner might always be checking up on you or posting things you don't want them to.

Or there could be a lack of respect when you are together – this could be emotional, physical or sexual harm, and all of these are always unacceptable. If you feel that there is a lack of respect in your relationship, or an abuse of power, talk to someone you know that you can trust.

Consent

Consent is crucial to a respectful relationship. When you give consent, you are giving the other person permission to go ahead with something. In a sexual situation, nothing should ever happen without your consent, and you can withdraw your consent at any point. Your partner should never continue to try having sex with you if you are not consenting (this could include being drunk or asleep). If they do continue without your consent, this is sexual assault or rape and they can be charged.

Consent: the facts

Consent is when a person gives permission for something to happen. Giving consent means that you know what is going to happen and are comfortable with it.

Sex and consent

When it comes to sex, consent is a legal requirement. This means that if consent isn't given, then the law is broken. Anyone involved in sexual activity must consent to it; freely, readily, and without any pressure whatsoever. Sexual activity includes touching, oral sex and intercourse. This law is designed to make sure that people have freedom over their own bodies and can make their own decisions about sex.

There are some important things to remember when thinking about consent to sex. Consent can only be given when there is a genuine choice. This means the people involved must agree by choice, and must have the freedom and capacity to make that choice. Freedom means the person is not pressured or manipulated into saying yes, and capacity means they fully understand and are able to make a clear decision. Being pressured or made to feel bad or unsafe means that consent has not been given as the person has not had a genuine choice. Similarly, if someone is really drunk they cannot give consent as they do not have capacity.

Consent can't be assumed and it is important to know that consent is not about listening out for a 'no '. Consent is about listening and asking for a 'yes ' to what is happening. Sometimes people don't consent to sexual stuff but don't use the word 'no '. They might be worried or scared to say it. Instead, they might use body language to communicate that they are not into it. Stopping kissing or touching, staying very still or avoiding physical contact can all be signs of non-consent. Don't ignore these signs - it's always best to ask a partner if they are okay. If they are happy with what is happening and if they want to carry on.

Have you seen the video comparing sexual consent to making someone a cup of tea? It's a funny and light-hearted way of showing that just as you wouldn't force someone to drink tea if they didn't want it – it is also wrong to force someone to have sex if they don't want it.

Consent and nudes:

According to the law, young people under the age of 18 cannot consent to a nude image of themselves being taken or shared with another person. However, from talking to young people we know that sometimes they do send 'nudes' to others. Young people tell us that they send nude selfies sometimes as part of a relationship or to peers, for fun or to feel good about themselves. Pics or videos are sometimes shared in a consensual way – both people may feel comfortable and want take and send the image.

However, there have been situations when nudes are shared without consent. Images might be shared through posting on social media, sending as part of a group chat or showing other people the image. Understandably, sharing nude images without consent can cause a lot of stress, embarrassment and anxiety for the young person involved. Sharing a nude image of someone else without them knowing is never okay and is against the law – whether you know the young person in the image or not.

Think before you share and remember that you can always take a stand. Telling an adult confidentially can help resolve the situation and make sure that the young person involved is supported. Reporting directly to the social media website/app can also help to remove the image if it has been posted online. If you need advice or someone to talk to about what you've seen, you can always speak confidentially to Childline at any time of the day.

Consent is not there if a person is pressured or emotionally blackmailed: If you are being made to feel bad for saying 'no' this means you don't have a genuine choice. Being made to feel you have to do something means that you haven't made the decision on your own without pressure – this isn't consent.

A person can't consent if their ability to make decisions is impaired: A person can't give consent if they are very drunk or under the influence of drugs. Drink and drugs can change your perspective on things and can affect your capacity to make decisions. Being encouraged to drink lots of alcohol or take drugs to make you more likely to have sex is never okay.

Consent cannot be given if a person is scared for their safety: If a person is threatened or made to feel unsafe for saying no, they cannot

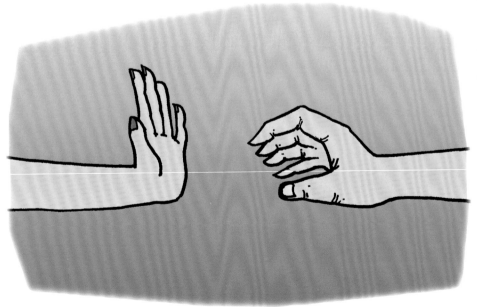

consent to sex. They may say yes or seem to go along with it – but this is not true consent. Consent can only be given if a personal feels safe and free to make a genuine choice.

Someone who is asleep or passed out cannot consent: It may seem obvious, but a person who is asleep or passed out cannot give permission to sexual activity. Even if they were awake and gave permission – if they fall asleep they can no longer make an informed decision.

Just because someone consents once, doesn't mean they always will: A person can give consent and change their mind at any point – even if sex has already begun. Carrying on once someone has changed their mind is rape. Consent needs to be given every time sexual activity takes place. Just because someone said yes once or even 100 times before – doesn't mean they consent every time.

If someone is under 16, they can't give consent: In UK law the age of consent is 16. This means that anyone below 16 cannot give consent even if they are saying yes to sex. Sex with anyone under 16 is illegal.

Always remember that no matter what your age, you don't have to say yes to things you don't want to do. You have the right to say no without an explanation. Someone that truly respects you will understand this.

Worried about consent or sex?

Talk to an adult that you trust (e.g. a parent/carer, teacher or youth worker) about what you're going through and get help.

The above information is reprinted with kind permission from Thinkuknow.
© Crown copyright 2019

www.thinkuknow.co.uk

About sexual violence - myths vs realities

There are lots of common myths about sexual violence, partly fuelled by poor media reporting.

Through our work, we know victims and survivors often have to deal with feelings of shame and guilt that can make it difficult to talk to anyone about what they've been through or get the help they want and need. Survivors also often fear others will blame them or they won't be believed. Sexual violence myths can reinforce these feelings and fears.

Rape Crisis is committed to dispelling myths and raising awareness and understanding of sexual violence.

Here are a few examples of common sexual violence myths:

Myth: Someone who's drunk lots of alcohol or taken drugs shouldn't complain if they end up being raped or sexually assaulted.

Fact: In law, consent to sex is when someone agrees by choice and has the freedom and capacity to make that choice. If a person is unconscious or incapacitated by alcohol or drugs, they are unable to give their consent to sex. Having sex with a person who is incapacitated through alcohol or drugs is rape. No-one asks or deserves to be raped or sexually assaulted; 100% of the responsibility lies with the perpetrator.

Myth: It's only rape if someone is physically forced into sex and has the injuries to show for it.

Fact: Sometimes people who are raped sustain injuries and sometimes they don't. Someone consents to sex when they agree by choice and have the freedom and capacity to make that choice. There are lots of circumstances in which someone might not have freedom or capacity to consent to sex. For example, rapists will sometimes use weapons or threats of violence to prevent a physical struggle. Sometimes they will take advantage of someone who isn't able to consent, because they are drunk or asleep. Many people who are sexually attacked are unable to move or speak from fear and shock. They may be in a coercive or controlling relationship with their rapist, and/or too young to give consent (under 16). Sex without consent is rape. Just because someone doesn't have visible injuries doesn't mean they weren't raped.

Myth: If two people have had sex with each other before, it's always OK to have sex again.

Fact: If a person is in a relationship with someone or has had sex with them before, it doesn't mean they can't be sexually assaulted or raped by that person. Consent must be given and received every time two people engage in sexual contact. It is important to check in with our sexual partners and make sure anything sexual that happens between us is what we both want, every time.

Myth: People who were sexually abused as children are likely to become abusers themselves.

Fact: This is a dangerous myth, which is sometimes used to try and explain or excuse the behaviour of those who rape and sexually abuse children. It is offensive and unhelpful to survivors of childhood sexual abuse. The vast majority of those who are sexually abused as children will never perpetrate sexual violence against others. There is no excuse or explanation for sexual violence against children or adults.

Myth: Women are most likely to be raped after dark by a stranger, so women shouldn't go out alone at night.

Fact: Only around 10% of rapes are committed by 'strangers'. Around 90% of rapes are committed by known men, and often by someone who the survivor has previously trusted or even loved. People are raped in their homes, their workplaces and other settings where they previously felt safe. Rapists can be friends, colleagues, clients, neighbours, family members, partners or exes. Risk of rape shouldn't be used as an excuse to control women's movements or restrict their rights and freedom.

Myth: People often lie about being raped because they regret having sex with someone or for attention.

Fact: Disproportionate media focus on false rape allegations can give the impression it's common for people to lie about sexual violence. This is not true. False allegations of rape are very rare. Most victims and survivors never report to the police. One reason for this is the fear of not being believed. It's really important we challenge this myth so those who've been through sexual violence can get the support and justice they need and deserve.

Myth: Only young, 'attractive' women and girls, who flirt and wear 'revealing' clothes, are raped.

Fact: People of all ages and appearances, and of all classes, cultures, abilities, genders, sexualities, races and religions, are raped. Rape is an act of violence and control; the perceived 'attractiveness' of a victim has very little to do with it. There is no excuse for sexual violence and it is never the victim/survivor's fault. What someone was wearing when they were raped is completely irrelevant.

Myth: Once a man is sexually aroused he can't help himself; he has to have sex.

Fact: Men can control their urges to have sex just as women can; no-one needs to rape someone for sexual satisfaction. Rape is an act of violence and control. It can't be explained away and there are no excuses.

Myth: When it comes to sex, women and girls sometimes 'play hard to get' and say 'no' when they really mean 'yes'.

Fact: Everyone has the legal right to say 'no' to sex and to change their mind about having sex at any point of sexual contact; if the other person doesn't stop, they are committing sexual assault or rape. When it comes to sex, we must respect the wishes of our sexual partner and believe what they tell us about what they do and don't want.

Myth: Alcohol, drugs, stress or depression can turn people into rapists.

Fact: Drugs and alcohol are never the cause of rape or sexual assault. It is the attacker who is committing the crime, not the drugs or alcohol. Stress and depression don't turn people into rapists or justify sexual violence either. There are no excuses.

Myth: Men of certain races and backgrounds are more likely to commit sexual violence.

Fact: There is no typical rapist. People who commit sexual violence come from every economic, ethnic, racial, age and social group.

Myth: Men don't get raped and women don't commit sexual offences.

Fact: The majority of sexual assaults and rapes are committed by men against women and children but women do perpetrate sexual violence. Often people who've been sexually assaulted or abused by a woman worry they won't be believed or their experiences won't be considered 'as bad'. This can make it difficult for these survivors to access services or justice.

Men are also raped and sexually assaulted. While Rape Crisis focuses particularly on the needs and rights of women and girl survivors, we of course recognise that the impacts of sexual violence on men and boys are no less devastating and we believe all survivors of sexual violence deserve specialist support.

In law, Rape is defined as non-consensual penetration with a penis. Non-consensual penetration with something other than a penis is defined as Sexual Assault by Penetration. For those who've experienced sexual violence that involved penetration by something other than a penis, whoever the perpetrator was, these legal definitions can feel restrictive, upsetting or insulting. **When we work with survivors, we are led by them, encourage them to name and frame their own experiences, and use the language they find most meaningful and reflexive of what they've been through, rather than strict legal terminology.**

The above information is reprinted with kind permission from Rape Crisis England & Wales.
© 2019 Rape Crisis England & Wales

www.rapecrisis.org.uk

Does the age of consent push people to have sex too soon?

Half of young women reported having a first sexual experience before they were 'competent'. Is it the fault of the law – or is it more complicated?

By Zoe Williams

The headline was enough to make you drop your marmalade: half of young women, and 43% of young men, said that they were not 'competent' when they lost their virginity, in a survey of nearly 3,000 17- to 24-year-olds released this week. If the idea of sexual competence strikes you as inherently droll, Melissa Palmer, who conducted the study as a research fellow at the London School of Hygiene & Tropical Medicine, helpfully subdivided it into four areas: consent, autonomy, contraceptive use and 'readiness'. The study looked only at heterosexual encounters.

Consent was measured by a three-option question about willingness: were you and your partner equally willing, were you more willing, were they more willing? This yielded the finding that nearly 20% of women felt less willing than their partner.

Autonomy depended on the circumstances of the encounter, which ranged from 'I was drunk/under the influence of drugs' and 'All my friends were doing it' to 'It felt like a natural follow-on' and 'I was in love'. Palmer notes: 'Those questions basically established whether the influencer was external to the self – peer pressure or alcohol – or internal to the self, driven by your own feelings.'

Contraceptive use is straightforward, and most young people – almost 90% – had used reliable contraception.

The question about readiness was: 'Thinking about the first time you had sex, was it about the right time, do you wish you had waited longer or do you wish you hadn't waited so long?' Just under 40% of women, and just over a quarter of men, did not feel they'd had sex for the first time at the right time. 'Very, very few wished it had been sooner,' Palmer says.

Only those respondents who answered positively in all four categories were deemed sexually competent. The report points out that there are implications beyond sexually transmitted infections and teenage pregnancies – which have been in steady decline for the past 20 years – for young people's wellbeing.

Does this mean the age of consent is too low? By definition it must be arbitrary, for as long as human beings are different, and mature at different rates, there can be no objective standard for sexual readiness. Self-evidently, though, an age of consent that would result in a pregnancy that would be physically harmful to the mother must be prioritising something other than the woman's wellbeing. For that reason, I would put 14 as too young, although that's the age of consent (at least for heterosexuals) in many countries, from Germany and Macedonia to Madagascar and Malawi. In South Korea, it is 13. 18 seems pretty stringent, though, and is far more common in Africa than in Europe. In the US, sexual consent laws vary from state to state, tending to put consent at 16 (though sometimes 17 or 18). Many states also

have 'Romeo and Juliet' laws, which reduce or eliminate penalties when parties are close in age.

Suffice to say, there is no direct correlation between what we would think of as the liberalism of a country and its age of consent, nor between the age of consent and the prevalence of sexual violence and/or gender discord, except at the extreme ends. Countries where the age of consent is 'at marriage' tend to have extremely high levels of violence against women and girls, although in the Democratic Republic of the Congo, the so-called rape capital of the world, the age of consent is 18 for males and 14 for females.

'The age of consent is a legal issue, which is something that we can't talk about as public health researchers,' Palmer says. 'The countries that have close-in-age type laws, so they don't focus on the age of young people but the age difference between partners, seem to take a more nuanced approach.'

Historically, the age of consent in Britain was ten or 12 until the end of the 19th century, but the concept of consent was so different – women having no sexual agency, marriage being taken as a blanket consent – that it's not comparable. The drive in the 1880s towards an age of consent of 16 was politically underpinned by the child labour elements of the factories acts of the previous two decades, which did more of the heavy lifting in terms of differentiating between adults and children than any moral, sexual crusade. And 16 is where the age of consent has stood since, only examined in recent memory as an equality issue when the age of gay consent was brought down from 18 to 16, in 2001.

So do these laws make any difference to the lived, regular experience of sex, or is their main use for the purpose of criminalising the exploitation of children? Palmer refers to some evidence – not from her own study – that having 16 as a legal age of consent 'can provide a useful safety net, in that people can say, "It's not legal", as a way of resisting pressure to have sex.' But it doesn't always work that way. Paula Hall is a sex therapist, and clinical director of the Laurel Centre. She says: 'I've heard a lot of young people say, "Rather than the age of consent, 16 is the deadline".'

In tandem with that pressure is the availability of porn. 'That becomes the easier option,' Hall says. 'You can have sexual experience without risk.' But there are things you could never learn from pornography. 'They don't have minor mishaps in porn. You rarely even see anyone put a condom on, and never the fiddly bit. Certainly in porn you do not see a guy losing his erection putting a condom on – it's all so seamless.'

Faced with these professional standards, some people are deferring actual sex for longer. 'A lot of the guys that I've worked with who use porn compulsively are still virgins at 23, 24, 28,' Hall says. 'The longer they've gone without a real-time partner, they start making out they've got more experience than they have, and they become absolutely terrified of it. They develop porn-induced erectile dysfunction. They worry about living up to the standards they see in pornography; they worry about losing their erection.'

The idea of people having sex when they are not autonomous, or not ready, suggests immediately the world of victims and culprits, but that's not what people describe. 'They're not necessarily a victim of someone else, but a victim of failure, a victim of their own insufficiency.'

Porn also interrupts the development of emotional readiness, if only because it never mentions it. 'There's a biological readiness, knowing your body is ready,' says Hall. 'But there's the psychological and the emotional bit as well. It has the potential to be the most wonderful, most amazing, most intimate encounter in the world. But it also has the potential to be really quite soul-destroying. It can make you feel fantastic or it can make you feel like shit, and are you ready to deal with either outcome?'

There's an answer that sounds a bit glib, which is: are you ever ready to have a sexual encounter with someone who doesn't care as much as you do? Is there any age at which that would be OK? And there's a very 21st-century answer, which is: don't let anyone do anything until they have hit full resilience, which is probably at about 35. Hall thinks the age of consent is a red herring. 'If we lowered the age of consent to 14 or upped it to 18 or 20, it wouldn't make the difference we think it would make. What matters is how we talk about sex to young people, and to each other.'

This article was amended on 24 January 2019. An earlier version said the Republic of Congo, where the age of consent is 18, had been called the 'rape capital of the world'; this name was actually used in reference to the neighbouring Democratic Republic of the Congo, where the age of consent is 18 for males and 14 for females. It was further amended on 7 February 2019 to correct the age of consent in South Korea from 20 to 13.

15 January 2019

Teenagers and single parents 'at highest risk of domestic abuse'

Teenage girls and single parents with children are among the most likely victims of domestic abuse, official data has revealed.

Figures published by the Office for National Statistics (ONS) has found that 7.6 per cent of 16- to 19-year-old girls had been the victim of abuse by a partner or ex-partner over the previous 12 months.

This is the largest proportion among all age groups, with the next largest (7.4 per cent) among 20- to 24-year-olds.

Among all women, 6.2 per cent said they had been the victim of abuse from a partner or ex-partner, which can include physical, emotional and financial abuse, threats of violence, sexual assault and stalking.

The data, which is based on surveys of women conducted between 2015 and 2017, also reveals that single parents are four times as likely to be a victim of domestic abuse than those living with other adults.

A fifth (20.5 per cent) of single women with children said they had experienced abuse from a partner in the previous 12 months, compared with 4.9 per cent among women living with other adults and children.

Single parents are also seven times as likely to have been stalked and three times as likely to have been the victim of sexual abuse by a partner or ex-partner.

'Today's analysis gives insight into the characteristics of women and girls who are more likely to experience partner abuse,' said Glenn Everett, ONS deputy director of wellbeing, inequalities, sustainability and environment.

'It also tells us about the types of households they live in. This can help to inform policies and services aimed at ending violence against women and girls – one of the key targets in the United Nations sustainable development goals.'

Earlier this week the charity Women's Aid and Queen Mary University of London released a report saying that children's lives are being put at risk as victims are being treated unfairly in court hearings.

Their research found that victims were repeatedly either not believed, blamed for abuse or seen as unstable by judges, barristers and Cafcass officers.

A consultation on measures to be included in the government's forthcoming domestic abuse bill closed this week.

In its response, Barnardo's is urging the government to improve support for children affected by domestic abuse, in particular in helping them address trauma.

'Barnardo's knows first-hand that children and young people are often the forgotten victims of domestic abuse. They are not just witnesses, even if abuse and violence isn't aimed directly at them,' said Barnardo's chief executive Javed Khan.

'Growing up in families where there is abuse or violence can lead to serious emotional effects which can stay with children for life.

'Research in our services shows many children who have been sexually exploited or who show harmful sexual behaviour live in households where there is abuse or violence. They are also more likely to be in abusive relationships themselves later in life.

'Children and young people need specialist support to overcome trauma and go on to lead happy, healthy lives and this bill is a missed opportunity to put them at the centre of their strategy.'

In December last year Ofsted criticised councils' response to domestic abuse. The inspectorate's annual report said that more needed to be done to tackle perpetrators and prevent abusive behaviour.

31 May 2018

This article was published originally in _Children & Young People Now_, the monthly magazine and website resource for children's services and youth sector professionals.
© MA Education 2019

www.cypnow.co.uk

Being loved, or being used?

Think about all your different relationships.

They could be with close friends, a boyfriend or girlfriend – and maybe groups of friends from school or the area you live in.

As we grow up, we develop relationships with lots of different people. It's how we learn what we enjoy about a relationship and what we don't.

But things can go wrong along the way and people might try to use you or force you to do something you don't want to do.

Sexual exploitation

Some people form relationships with young people to use them for sex.

People who do this want young people to think they are a friend, or a boyfriend or girlfriend. They want to gain their trust to get power over them. They might also use bribes, threats, humiliation and even violence to get power over them.

They use that power to force them to have sex, or do sexual things, with them and sometimes with other people. This is sexual exploitation and it's a crime.

It happens to boys and girls and can be really hard to spot. Often people think they're in a good relationship, even after things have turned bad.

But there are warning signs. It's really important that you know how to spot them so you can protect yourself and your friends.

Met someone new? Five signs they are not all they seem

It can be hard to spot when someone is using you. Here are some possible signs:

1. To get to know you they give you lots of attention.

We all like attention and it's nice to feel wanted. But if someone tries to get to know you by giving you lots of attention, ask yourself – what do they really want?

2. They give you gifts, like phone credit, alcohol, drugs or jewellery.

This can be exciting and make you feel good about someone but if they want sex in return they are trying to exploit you.

3. They try to isolate you from your friends or family.

They will say that they are the only person you need. They might tell you that your friends or family won't understand or you'll be in trouble. Remember, the people who care about you will want to protect you.

4. They have mood swings.

If someone flips between being 'very nice' and 'very nasty', you can feel like you need to do things to keep them happy. This can be a sign they are trying to control you.

5. They control you with promises and threats.

Abusers use many tricks to control young people. They may make promises they can't keep, ask them to keep secrets or threaten them. Some become violent.

Safer relationships

It's really important you feel safe in any relationship you're in.

- **Trust yourself to know when something is wrong.** If someone makes you feel unsafe, pressured or frightened, follow your instincts and get help.

- **Consider whether you can trust people you don't know.** Even if they seem friendly, exciting or offer you gifts. Ask yourself – why are they being nice and doing me favours? What do they want in return?

- **You don't have to do things that you think are unsafe.** If you feel nervous about doing something, try to find a way out of the situation and seek help from someone you trust.

- **You should never be put under pressure to have sex.** If someone really cares about you they won't put any pressure on you. If you don't feel you can say no, ask yourself, are you really in a safe situation?

- **Know where to get help.** Keep contact details of an adult you trust with you, written down and on your phone. Keep your phone topped up with credit.

Are you worried you're being exploited?

If you are worried about a situation that you, or a friend, is in you should talk to an adult you trust as soon as you can. People who can help include parents, teachers, police officers social workers and youth workers.

Love Island: Adam shows teenagers how not to treat romantic partners

An article from The Conversation.

THE CONVERSATION

By Janette Porter, Sessional Lecturer, Liverpool John Moores University and Kay Standing, Reader in Gender Studies, Liverpool John Moores University

Adam's manipulative behaviour towards the women he likes in the *Love Island* villa prompted charity Women's Aid to issue a statement asking viewers to join love interest Rosie in speaking out against unhealthy behaviours in relationships – especially 'gaslighting ', a form of emotional abuse that makes someone question their own feelings, memories and version of reality.

Emotional partner abuse is a common experience among young people. Research shows that nearly three quarters of teenage girls, and half of teenage boys, have reported some form of emotional partner abuse. But many still won't recognise the early warning signs, and only 33% of teenagers who are involved in an abusive relationship talk to someone about it.

Although the UK's legal definition of domestic violence and abuse includes psychological abuse and controlling and coercive behaviour, research by child protection charity NSPCC has shown that teenagers often don't understand what emotional abuse is, and how controlling behaviours – such as checking someone's phone, telling them what to wear or gaslighting – can be early warning signs of abusive behaviour.

Love Island is watched by over three million viewers and most are young women aged 16 to 34, though a younger teenage demographic also watch. Many of these younger viewers may be learning about what healthy relationships are like, and entering their first romantic relationship.

If young people are getting their information about relationships from programmes such as *Love Island* – with emotional abuse as entertainment – they will inevitably have trouble recognising the early warning signs of abuse, as they might think that this type of relationship is normal. There is a clear need to help young people recognise abuse in relationships, and fight back against it.

Let's teach about sex

In the past, government strategies to promote healthy relationships – including Disrespect Nobody and This is Abuse – have targeted 13- to 18-year-olds with extensive media campaigns. These strategies recognised the power of TV, celebrities and social media to influence young people's views of relationships. For example, This is Abuse partnered with the Channel 4 teen soap *Hollyoaks* in 2013.

One in four teenagers admit they are more influenced by celebrities than people they know. This is why there needs to be positive role models of healthy relationships in the media. But evidence shows that domestic abuse can also be prevented through early, age-appropriate education, which promotes relationships based on equality and respect.

Currently, relationship and sex education is not compulsory. But from September 2019, it will be a statutory requirement in all schools. In order to be effective, high-quality relationship and sex education needs to start early, in order to influence attitudes and behaviours before they are entrenched in adulthood. It needs to be about rights and equity, and delivered by either well-trained teachers, or external professionals.

Drama lessons

At Liverpool John Moores University, we are working with arts charity Tender to prevent domestic abuse by using art and drama in 24 schools across Greater Merseyside. Using age- and ability-appropriate workshops, which focus on identifying early warning signs in unhealthy relationships, young people are encouraged to question past relationship behaviours and challenge their current norm.

The PEACH study (Preventing Domestic Abuse for Children) has proven that drama is a particularly effective way of teaching pupils how to recognise the early warning signs of abusive relationships. One female pupil, aged 14, said: '*I used to think it as OK for my boyfriend to log into my Facebook account but I know now it's not*'.

People's understanding of what is a healthy and unhealthy relationship comes from many sources, including family, friends, peers, the media and school. We expect that society will offer models of healthy relationships and portray positive intimate partner relationships. But that is not always the case, as *Love Island* shows.

Rosie called out Adam's behaviour, and it's time we enable everyone to do the same. Schools have a responsibility to provide young people with the skills and information to recognise the signs of unhealthy relationships, and speak out against abuse.

25 June 2019

How to get over a break-up, according to psychology

Studies show that the brain responds to heartbreak like addicts experiencing cocaine withdrawal.

By Olivia Petter

There's no way to sugar-coat it, break-ups are rough. Sure, you can bitch and moan about your ex and chant self-love mantras till the cows come home – but there's no denying the unbearable pain of parting ways with someone you once loved.

However, how long that pain lingers is ultimately up to you, explains psychologist Guy Winch, whose book, *How to Fix a Broken Heart,* debunks some common myths surrounding heartbreak.

While popular culture might have you believe that a new part-time lover and a perpetual supply of Ben & Jerry's is all you need to move on, Winch explains that break-ups affect us far more severely than we realise.

'Functional MRI brain scan studies have shown that the withdrawal of romantic love activates the same mechanisms in the brain as get activated when addicts go through withdrawal from substances like cocaine or opioids,' the TED speaker told *The Independent*.

'In other words, love is addictive and heartbreak causes us to go through powerful withdrawal.'

This, Winch explains, is why we obsess over our ex partners to the point where we feel we crave them as if they were a drug we have been deprived of.

This is also why it can be so hard to move onto someone else, he adds, because we're inclined to idealise our exes to the nth degree, consequently distorting our memories of them by convincing ourselves that our romanticised vision of them is an accurate one, when most of the time it is not.

'You have to make sure that any thoughts you have about an ex are realistic and balanced,' Winch insists.

'If your mind conjures up images of your happiest weekend together, you need to add in the images from the weekend that drove you crazy and upset you tremendously.

'If you find yourself longing for their sweet embrace, you should remember the nights they rejected our advances and slept on the far edge of the bed.'

For those really struggling to get to grips with reality, Winch suggests writing down a list of all the reasons why the relationship didn't work.

Another tricky aspect of heartbreak can be reckoning with the idea of 'being dumped' and spending your days in a hole of self-pity while the person who did the 'dumping' is back out there living his or her best life without you.

Why is it so much harder to be broken up with than to break-up with someone yourself?

The answer might seem obvious, but Winch explains it's crucial to fully understand this dissonance in order to fully 'recover'.

While the break-up might seem sudden to the person who has just been dumped, Winch explains that their partner has probably been emotionally disengaged in the relationship for a long time.

'By the time the break-up happens, they are essentially over the relationship,' he said.

'However, the person who got dumped is just finding out and is in the most initial stages of grief and loss.

'People often find it bewildering that their ex was so normal and loving one week only to break-up with them the next. But the ex was only acting loving, because they hadn't decided to 'pull the plug' yet, they weren't actually feeling that way.'

When it comes to tackling heartbreak, Winch adds that there are a number of common traps people fall into.

Here, the author gives his top six tips to avoiding these and start your road to recovery ASAP.

1. Do NOT check up on them on social media. This will reinforce your ex's presence in your mind and only make it harder for you to stop fantasising about your broken relationship.
2. Avoid creating mysteries about why the break-up happened, this will give your ex a starring role in your thoughts when you need to downgrade them to an extra. Accept any explanation that fits the facts and keeps your self-esteem intact such as they were unwilling to commit, they allowed themselves to drift emotionally and didn't bring up what was happening until it was too late, or they were just not the person you thought they were.
3. Make a list of all of the compromises you had to make in the relationship that you would rather not make next time.
4. Do the things that used to bring you enjoyment and interest even if they don't seem interesting and enjoyable now. Going through the motions is an important way to signal to yourself that life goes on.
5. Remove reminders of the relationship that cause you distress or pain such as texts and photographs.
6. Reach out to friends and make the most of their support; heartbreak is ubiquitous and everybody has their own words of wisdom to offer.

20 March 2019

Splitting up

Feel like it's not working out?

Relationships come in all shapes and sizes, and they all have their ups and downs. Some only last a short time, while others can be long term. But sometimes in a relationship one or both people realise, that for any number of different reasons, it just isn't working out. Ending a relationship is often very difficult for both people, particularly if you care about the other person's feelings. Being on the receiving end of a break-up can feel even more heart-breaking.

Need to end it?

If you're unhappy in a relationship, remember your feelings count, and it's your responsibility to say so. It may feel kinder to let things go on but in the long run the other person may end up being more hurt. So choose a good time to tell the person. It may be that a quiet space is best, or that having other people around may work better. Try to treat them the same way you would like to be treated if you were in their shoes.

It may feel horrible for a while, or it may feel good to have ended a relationship that wasn't making you happy. The other person may be relieved it's ended too. So don't give yourself a hard time. If you're feeling low at the end of a relationship, spend time doing whatever makes you feel good about yourself – being with friends, exercise and hobbies can all help.

Been dumped?

It can feel like the worst thing in the world to be dumped, especially if you still have strong feelings for the person and want the relationship to continue. Realising they don't feel the same as you can be very hard on your self-confidence too.

If you are struggling after the end of a relationship try and do things that make you feel better about yourself – spend time with friends that cheer you up, try reading a self-help book, call a helpline to talk it through (e.g., Breathing Space on 0800 83 85 87) or visit an accredited service and talk to a professional in confidence). Remember also that exercise releases natural chemicals into your body that can actually make you feel better.

It's okay to hide away for a while if that's how you feel, but don't forget, it's fine to be single. Being dumped may feel awful for a while, but it won't always feel this bad – things will get better. So try and focus on making yourself happy for a while.

'Revenge porn'

Some young people have been affected by this. This is when a partner or ex has sexual images of you that you maybe agreed to at the time, but they are now using them to threaten you because you want to split, or you've already broken up and they have posted the pictures to get back at you.

This is abuse and you do not have to put up with it. Tell someone you trust.

Key facts

- In 2017, the first age at which more than 50% of young people had left the parental home was 23. (page 1)

- In 2016, the average age of a first-time mother was 29 – two years later than it was in 1997. (page 1)

- In the UK today, people in their 20s are more likely to have children than be married, with the average age of first-time marriage increasing in 2015 to 33 for men and 31 for women. (page 1)

- In 1993, the average house price was 4.9 times the average household salary of a household headed by a 16- to 24-year-old. In 2016, it was 8.2 times (a decline from its peak of 11.2 times in 2007). (page 2)

- The average cost of a wedding in the UK is over £20,000. (page 3)

- Almost half of unmarried couples who live together mistakenly believe they share the same rights as couples who have tied the knot. (page 6)

- Cohabiting couples account for the fastest growing type of household in England and Wales. (page 6)

- The number of opposite-sex cohabiting couple families with dependent children has more than doubled in the last decade. (page 6)

- 41% of respondents were aware that there is no common-law marriage between cohabiting couples, with more than half of households with children believing that unmarried couples shared the same rights as those who are married. (page 6)

- According to the Office of National Statistics, there were 106,959 divorces of opposite-sex couples in 2016 in England and Wales. (page 6)

- 112 same-sex couples were divorced in 2016; of these 78% were female couples. (page 6)

- Cohabiting couples (both opposite and same-sex couples) are the fastest growing type of family, more than doubling from 1.5 million families in 1996 to 3.3 million families in 2017. (page 7)

- In England and Wales, cohabitants have no legal status and, therefore, no automatic rights. (page 7)

- In 2006, Scotland introduced a set of limited rights for cohabitants who separate, or in cases where one partner dies. (page 7)

- The proportion of children aged 10 to 15 years who argued more than once a week with their mother fell significantly from 30.5% in 2009 to 2010 to 25.8% in 2015 to 2016. (page 9)

- The proportion of children aged 10 to 15 years reporting high or very high happiness with friends fell significantly from 85.8% in 2015 to 80.5% in 2017, with boys being the main driver of this change. (page 9)

- There is no evidence of a negative impact of living in a single parent household on children's wellbeing in terms of their self-reported life satisfaction, quality of peer relationships, or positivity about family life. (page 11)

- Sibling bullying does have an impact on mental health later in life. (page 14)

- Psychological bullying was the most reported type of bullying, and males bullied their siblings more often than females. (page 14)

- Those aged 18 to 24 are the demographic most likely to be spending the holidays with their parents (77%). (page 15)

- The presence of children in the house makes an argument 40% more likely: 38% with a child in the house foresee a Christmas row, compared to 26% of those in childless households. (page 15)

- Girls are nearly twice as likely to have arguments with both their mother and father over their clothes. (page 16)

- Boys were also more likely to have arguments with their mothers over homework. (page 16)

- 83% of teenagers questioned said they never argued with grandparents. (page 16)

- Adults who had imaginary friends, meanwhile, report that they are more creative and imaginative than those who did not. (page 18)

- Research has shown that talking to yourself can be a sign of high cognitive functioning and creativity. (page 18)

- The longer you spend with someone, the more likely you are to develop a close bond with them. (page 19)

- The majority of us are closest to just five people and call about 15 people good friends while 150 is the estimated limit for how many relationships the brain can handle overall. (page 19)

- 51 per cent of the public say chatting to friends "in real life" is unnecessary because they are kept up to date on what people are up to via social media. (page 20)

- A poll of 5,000 adults across the UK found the average person has 770 friends on social media. (page 20)

- Those aged 18 to 24 are around 20 times more likely to never speak to their neighbours, than those aged 55 and over. (page 20)

- Only around 10% of rapes are committed by 'strangers'. Around 90% of rapes are committed by known men. (page 32)

- Just under 40% of women, and just over a quarter of men, did not feel they'd had sex for the first time at the right time. (page 33)

- 7.6 per cent of 16- to 19-year-old girls had been the victim of abuse by a partner or ex-partner over the previous 12 months. (page 35)

- One in four teenagers admit they are more influenced by celebrities than people they know. (page 37)

Glossary

Civil partnership

Civil partnership allows same-sex couples to obtain essentially the same rights and responsibilities as civil marriage. Civil partnership can be converted to a marriage.

Civil partnership dissolution

Similar to a divorce, civil partnership dissolution is the legal ending of the civil partnership. The grounds for dissolution are unreasonable behaviour, separation, and desertion.

Cohabiting couple

Two people who live together as a couple but are not married or in a civil partnership. Current trends suggest more couples are choosing to have children in cohabiting rather than married relationships.

Common-law marriage

Many people believe that a marriage-like relationship can be established simply by cohabiting for an extended period of time. In legal terms, this is not true. Cohabitation does not lead to the same rights as marriage.

Consent

The act of giving permission for something to happen. This can include medical consent- such as giving permission for a medical procedure to be carried out, or sexual consent – to give permission to a partner to take part in a sexual act.

Contraception

Anything which prevents conception, or pregnancy, from taking place. 'Barrier methods', such as condoms, work by stopping sperm from reaching an egg during intercourse and are also effective in preventing sexually transmitted infections (STI's). Hormonal methods such as the contraceptive pill change the way a woman's body works to prevent an egg from being fertilised. Emergency contraception, commonly known as the 'morning-after pill', is used after unprotected sex to prevent a fertilised egg from becoming implanted in the womb.

Digital abuse

Most frequently occurring in teenage relationships, digital abuse involves the use of texting and social networking sites to keep track of, harass, stalk, control, bully or intimidate a partner.

Divorce

The legal ending of a marriage after a permanent breakdown of the relationship. Grounds for divorce include adultery, unreasonable behaviour, separation and desertion.

Family

A domestic group related by blood, marriage or other familial ties living together in a household. A 'traditional' or nuclear family usually refers to one in which a married heterosexual couple raise their biological children together; however, changing family structures has resulted in so-called 'non-traditional' family groups including step-families, families with adopted or foster children, single-parent families and children being raised by same-sex parents.

Lone/single parent

Someone who is raising a child alone, either due to divorce/separation, widowhood, an absent parent or due to single adoption. The majority of lone parents are women.

Marriage

In the UK, the legal age at which you can marry is 18-years-old, or 16- to 17-years-old if you have parental consent. In England, Wales and Scotland same-sex couples can also marry. As yet in Northern Ireland same-sex marriage is not allowed.

Rape

Forcing someone to engage in sexual intercourse against their will. Force is not necessarily physical, it could also be emotional or psychological.

Risky Behaviour

Behaviour that has the potential to get out of control or become dangerous.

Safe sex

Being safe with sex means caring for both your own health, and the health of your partner. Being safe protects you from getting or passing on STIs and from unplanned pregnancy.

Sexting

Someone uploading and sending an indecent, usually sexually graphic, image to their friend or boy/girlfriend via mobile phone or the Internet.

Sexual abuse

Sexual abuse occurs when a victim is forced into a sexual act against their will, through violence or intimidation. This can include rape. Sexual abuse is always a crime, no matter what the relationship is between the victim and perpetrator.

Sexual bullying

This includes a range of behaviours such as sexualised name-calling and verbal abuse, mocking someone's sexual performance, ridiculing physical appearance, criticising sexual behaviour, spreading rumours about someone's sexuality or about sexual experiences they have had or not had, unwanted touching and physical assault. Sexual bullying is behaviour which is repeated over time and intends to victimise someone by using their gender, sexuality or sexual (in)experience to hurt them.

Social media

Media which are designed specifically for electronic communication. 'Social networking' websites allow users to interact using instant messaging, share information, photos and videos and ultimately create an online community. Examples include Facebook, LinkedIn and micro-blogging site Twitter.

Step-family

Step-families come together when people marry again or live with a new partner. This may be after the death of one parent, separation or divorce. It can also mean that children from different families end up living together for all or part of the time. One in four children has parents who get divorced and over half of their mothers and fathers will remarry or repartner to form a step-family.

Assignments

Brainstorming

- In small groups, discuss what you know about relationships. Consider the following points:
  - What is a family? Is there just one definition, or are there many different types?
  - How can you tell if someone is a good friend?
  - Would you recognise the signs that someone is in an abusive relationship?
- In pairs, write a pro-con list for getting married or having a civil partnership.
- Create a Diamond Nine on the topic of friendship. List the most important factors down to the least important on being a good friend.

Research

- Create a questionnaire to find out how often, and why your friends argue with their parents or siblings. Is there any differences in the topics argued about between parents or siblings? Create a graph to show your findings.
- Read the article 'Social media updates "killing conversations" between friends' on page 20 and create a questionnaire to find out whether your classmate speak to their friends more face-to-face or by social media. Write a short summary and feedback to your class.
- Read the article 'Children's wellbeing and social relationships, UK: 2018' and do some further research on the topic. Write a short report of your findings.
- Do some research on ways to make new friends. Create a PowerPoint or Prezi presentation with your ideas.

Design

- Design a poster to explain sexual consent.
- Choose one of the articles in this book and create an illustration to highlight the key themes/message of your chosen article.
- Design a leaflet to help teens get over a break-up.
- Design a website/app to help people find new friends.
- Imagine you work for a charity that promotes healthy relationships. Design a campaign to raise awareness of unhealthy relationships. Your campaign could include posters, TV adverts, radio adverts, social media marketing or website banners.
- Design a poster on peer-pressure. Consider how to spot the signs that someone is being pressured into doing something that they don't want to do.

Oral

- As a class, discuss healthy relationships. Consider how you can tell whether a relationship is healthy or not.
- In pairs, discuss how you can be a good friend.
- In pairs, discuss the ways that you can get over a relationship break-up. This can be either a romantic relationship or a friendship.
- In small groups, discuss whether civil partnerships should be available to mixed-sex couples.
- As a class, discuss consent.
- As a class, discuss your thoughts on arguing with your parents.

Reading/writing

- Read *The Perks of Being a Wallflower* by Stephen Chbosky and write a review exploring how the author deals with the theme of friendship.
- Write a blog post about frenemies.
- Write a one-paragraph definition of consent.
- Read the article 'Milestones: journeying into adulthood' on page 1 and write a summary for your school newspaper.
- Write a diary entry from the perspective of a child experiencing sibling bullying. Consider how their parents would react when told of what is happening.
- Write a short story about someone who is feeling pressure from a friend or partner to do something that they don't want to do.
- Write a letter to an Agony Aunt/Uncle with a relationship problem. Be imaginative – consider the different types of problems that your age-group may encounter. Then write a short reply offering advice on how to deal with the situation.

Acknowledgements

The publisher is grateful for permission to reproduce the material in this book. While every care has been taken to trace and acknowledge copyright, the publisher tenders its apology for any accidental infringement or where copyright has proved untraceable. The publisher would be pleased to come to a suitable arrangement in any such case with the rightful owner.

Images

All images courtesy of iStock except pages 4, 5, 7, 12, 17, 27, 35: Pixabay, 8, 13, 14, 24, 31, 32, 33: Unsplash, 20, 26, 29, 34, 36: Rawpixel.

Illustrations

Don Hatcher: pages 30 & 39. Simon Kneebone: pages 25 & 28. Angelo Madrid: pages 8 & 15.

Additional acknowledgements

With thanks to Rape Crisis England & Wales, authors of the article on pages 31 & 32.

With thanks to the Independence team: Shelley Baldry, Danielle Lobban, Jackie Staines and Jan Sunderland.

Tracy Biram

Cambridge, May 2019